The Haunting Of Natalie Bradford: Part I

Based on a true story.

BOOKS BY L. SYDNEY FISHER

STANDALONES
See No Evil
The Devil's Board

The Phoenix Series
The Phoenix Mission, Part I
The Phoenix Codes, Part II

The Bradford Series
The Haunting of Natalie Bradford, Part I
The Haunting of Natalie Bradford, Part II:
Waking the Dead
The Haunted Prophecy of Natalie Bradford:
The Complete Bradford Series

The Haunted
Volume I, The Devil's Den
Volume II, The Wilderness
Volume III, Possum Town
Volume IV, On The Haunted Trail

Author's Note

All names and some locations have been changed in this book for the sake of privacy and out of respect for the deceased. The Haunting of Natalie Bradford was inspired by a true story. When appropriate, the author has dramatized some scenes in this book for the sake of storytelling.

Editing provided by: Kathleen H. McCormick

Hardcover Edition:
ISBN: 978-0-9991440-0-8

Paperback Edition:
ISBN-13: 9780692305218
ISBN-10: 0692305211

Published by: Legacy Books Unlimited, Inc.
Cover Design: L. Sydney Fisher

For Hannah,
My answered prayer.

FOREWORD

I began my research twenty-five years after Liz Bradford's death. Unknown to me, there was a hidden story within a story. The synchronistic findings were incredulous, and I found myself bewildered as I uncovered a prophecy that seemed to be predestined for Natalie Houston. Was she simply in the wrong place at the wrong time? Or, was she being used as an instrument to reveal a prophetic message?

My research carried me to the graveyard where Liz Bradford had been buried. I looked all around, not knowing which way to go. I closed my eyes and concentrated on the area while listening for my sixth sense to guide me. I then opened my eyes and walked directly to the site where Liz Bradford lay! A new tombstone was laid on Ms. Bradford's grave. It was larger than the old one I remembered, and it had an inscription.

Trees had grown to maturity from the hillside gravesite hiding the front view of an abandoned Lindenwood. The grass seemed to be greener and thicker than it was years ago, and I noticed a new bouquet of flowers resting at her headstone. I will never forget the uneasiness that swept over me as I stood in the same place where I had stood twenty-five years before.

Later, my research took me to the courthouse in search of the court records from Devon Bradford's trial. It took almost three weeks to locate the transcripts. Of all the files in the room, the Bradford case had mysteriously been misfiled in a box stacked out of place. I wondered if someone was trying to warn me to stay away. Each day I sat in the small, crowded storage room of the courthouse and studied the transcripts as if I was in a hypnotic trance. The more I read, the more scared I became. My research continued to turn up more and more bizarre coincidences that sent chills creeping up my back.

A few months after the first draft of this book was written, I came in contact with the bartender on duty the night Liz Bradford was murdered. During my interview with him, he told me that Liz Bradford's suitcase sat packed just inside his stepfather's office door. He said it sat there for many weeks, maybe even months. I was saddened for her. She never came back to pick it up.

Years later, I found myself living in a house behind The Rex Plaza where Liz Bradford was murdered. Not knowing the history of the house, my husband and I bought it as an investment and later found out it was haunted. I still do not know the origin of the spirit, but I can promise you, it scared the hell out of me. We lived there five years. Many days I sat on my redwood deck in the backyard of my home and gazed across the fence at the parking lot of the prestigious motel. I daydreamed of the days Liz Bradford once walked the floors of the lavishly decorated lounge serving cocktails to the wealthy guests and out of town patrons looking for some nightlife in Elvis's town.

I still visit the restaurant where she worked and try to imagine myself as a customer on the night she died. The parking lot and facility is still standing in the same structure it was 38 years ago. The spirit of Liz Bradford is still prevalent to me when I walk in the restaurant.

Today, I live in a house that is ghost free. After many years of extensive study and dealing with the paranormal, I have to say I don't miss the unnerving chaos that ghosts can cause, but some ghosts such as the spirit of Liz Bradford need us to tell their stories. Sometimes, the person they pick to tell the story may not be a coincidence. Natalie Houston was a non-believer in the spiritual world, but she got an introduction that would change her thinking for the rest of her life and her sleep.

Sweet Dreams, Natalie.

To Liz and Natalie,
may you both rest in peace.

CHAPTER 1

Liz Bradford wrestled against the stinging blows of her husband's hands. Tiny strands of dark brown hair lay scattered across the floor as Devon Bradford ripped them loose from her head. She cried out in pain.

"Stop!" She slapped at him only causing his fury to accelerate.

"If I can't have you, nobody will!" Devon shouted.

Liz moaned and forced herself out of the bedroom door. Devon picked up a nearby belt and began beating her with it. Swinging wildly as the leather snapped against her skin.

"Leave me alone! Stop!" She begged.

Devon stood over her staring at her with a loathing that promised deadly consequences if she left him. He wouldn't allow it. His mind was made up. He turned and walked away as Liz climbed onto the living room sofa.

She massaged the tender bruises and stinging pain on her face and head. She closed her eyes and vowed that she would escape tomorrow. She silently made her plans. When morning came, she would quickly get her things and drive to a friend's house in Tupelo. He wouldn't follow her there. If she could get away long enough, maybe she could figure out what she needed to do. Although her husband had accused her of seeing other men, she felt her marriage had been over for some time. People didn't know the man she knew.

Love had not been kind here, but would it be kind somewhere else? If she stayed, she might never know, but what would be the consequences of leaving? Liz began to drift to sleep. Hours seemed to pass like minutes. Liz awakened to find a calm silence within the house. The children were still sleeping as she hurriedly shoved piles of clothes into the truck. She had not seen Devon and wasn't about to concern herself with his whereabouts. It was time to leave before he returned.

She rushed up the stairs and walked to the side of her daughter's bed. Liz quickly sat down next to Susan gently shaking her awake.

Susan stirred. She rubbed her eyes and squinted at her mother. "What? What is it?"

Liz paused looking at her daughter. She felt an overwhelming sense of dread. "Honey, I just wanted to say Good-bye. This may be the last time that I see you."

Susan looked at her mother with disbelief. She leaned up and hugged her unaware of the reality in Liz's statement.

Liz Bradford turned and walked out the door. She was consumed with angst. Somehow she sensed that this day was the beginning of the end. Was it fear consuming her or the uncanny essence of premonition? She was unknowingly casting a spell of events beyond her control. It was now just a matter of hours before a prophecy would be born.

✝

CHAPTER 2

Liz Bradford stepped onto the front lawn of her friend and co-worker, Rose Smith. She slammed the truck door shut. She had filled the front seat with clothes and a .25 mm handgun. Her feet seemed to skip as she neared the front door. Rose Smith was waiting for her on the front steps of her home.

"Oh, Liz. What has he done to you?" Rose reached for Liz's hand and beckoned for her to come inside.

"Nothing more than he usually does, but this time I've had enough. I mean it. I swear I'm not going back to him." Liz rubbed her fingers across the bruises that surrounded her neck and head. Bald patches covered various places about her head where Devon Bradford had pulled and stripped away her hair.

Rose shook her head in disbelief. She had heard that story before. How many times had she seen Liz Bradford shaken by a situation she didn't know how to escape from?

"All I've got to say is you're crazy if you do."

Rose looked tiny next to Liz's 5'7" frame. She led Liz to the living room where she invited her to sit down. She stopped in the kitchen and poured two cups of coffee before joining her.

Liz sighed. "You know, I've spent years with Devon, but I can't stand it anymore." Her eyes were misty as she put the hot coffee to her lips.

Liz cleared her throat. She wiped the corners of her eyes. Then just as quick, her expression changed into a vengeful stare. Her eyes focused on her friend, her lips pursed together. Her fingers curled tighter around the cup's handle. She thought about the night before when Devon had beat her head with his fists, his fury gaining momentum with each blow. He had left his humiliating tattoos on her for the last time.

"Rose, if you don't care, I want to stay here until I have to go to work this afternoon." Liz's eyes were glassy.

Rose nodded in agreement. "Of course you can."

"I said I wasn't going back. If he hurts me again, I swear I'll kill him."

Rose stared at her friend with unease. "I think you are in over your head, Liz. He may kill *you*. He's already told you he would."

Liz trembled. "I have a gun in the truck." She turned her eyes away and quickly looked back at Rose.

If he kills me, I'll come back for that bastard. I'll curse him for the rest of his life."

Rose felt a coldness sweep over her. Her stomach churned as she sat back in her chair. There was no more doubting what might be coming. She now feared for Liz's life.

***

Meanwhile, Devon Bradford contemplated the day's events. His wife had packed her clothes and left, but she would be back. He was sure of it. If she refused, he would surely kill her. She would not humiliate him or disrespect him by leaving. Especially for another man.

He lifted the hood on the pale blue Chevy Impala. He busied himself with routine maintenance and repairs on the family's vehicle. Devon had a way of seeming taller than he actually was. At near 6'0, he exuded a presence unlike other men. He was a master of disguise leaving some women enchanted by his charisma and striking good looks. Devon stood back and stretched. The white cotton shirt often referred to as a 'wifebeater' that he frequently wore was soiled with oil and grime. He tossed the cigarette butt he had been gripping in his teeth to the ground. It was getting late. Liz would be going to work and he would be joining her just before midnight. In less than six hours, the stage would be set and the drama would include a whole new cast of characters in her story.

CHAPTER 3

December 21st, 1974, approximately 11:30 p.m.

Liz Bradford swung her hands in the air as the stinging blows swept across her face. She cried out with each blow, her head and neck still tender from the night before. Her butler style uniform of black and white satin was wrinkled and soiled with splotches of blood that dripped from her nose. She was fighting a battle she was sure to lose, but she was determined to leave Devon Bradford and his controlling ways. She had made up her mind, and nothing he could say or do was going to stop her.

The parking lot of the glamorous Rex Plaza was almost empty. Only the streetlights glowed in the foreground of the white brick motel, and the nautical style brass lanterns hanging outside the front door cast a soft light on the lot. The motel's guests were quiet in their rooms with few lights still shining through the curtains. The faint sound of Elvis Presley's *Jailhouse Rock* could be heard just outside the front door to the lounge known as The Lion's Den. No one inside the motel could hear Liz's screams, and there was no one outside to stop Devon Bradford.

Liz dropped her cigarette. Her hair was being ripped from her head. She kept swinging her long slender arms and hands in front of her face desperately trying to block the blows, but she wasn't strong enough. She felt his hands tightening around her neck. Her mind raced as the breath was being choked from her lungs. She struggled with a force greater than she ever had before. He couldn't get away with this any longer. How many times had she narrowly escaped strangulation? She gasped for air and felt the heat rise in her face as her chestnut eyes began to water. Still slinging her arms about, she swept her hands across the seat beside her to find the .25 caliber pistol she had been carrying. She swung it around, but Devon was too quick. His hands were on the barrel pulling the gun from her grip. Liz screamed out. She twisted her body quickly as she got on her knees and began to climb in the backseat of the Chevy Impala. If she didn't escape fast, he would kill her. Her feet scraped the dashboard of the car as she maneuvered herself over the seat. Time seemed to stand still as fear paralyzed her movements. She felt herself moving in slow motion. She whimpered, mouthing words to herself.

"No, No. This can't-"

"Bitch!" Devon Bradford's icy blue eyes were filled with rage, his mouth clenched as he struck her.

Hate and jealously fueled his fury as he gripped the 25 mm pistol. He wouldn't let her get away with the humiliation she had caused him. She would not make a fool out of him in his own hometown. The thought of his wife being with another man was too much for his ego. He had an image he had to uphold. Everyone in the community knew Devon Bradford. He was the reason all of Liz's friends envied her.

Liz screamed. She heard only one shot. Fleeting memories passed through her mind like a movie reel. Her eyes began to close as she screamed in silence one last time in an effort to awaken from a nightmare that would not end. Her body suddenly became limp from the sharp stabbing pains in her back. Saliva began to ooze out of her mouth as tears spilled from her eyes and mucus dripped from her long slender nose. Streaks of mascara ran down her face that had been carefully painted with dark, pink rouge and red lipstick for her night's work as a waitress at the classiest restaurant in town. Her head lay over the front seat facing the back windshield. Another shot rang out. With the second shot, Liz Bradford was dead.

"Central to Baker Three." The urgency in the dispatcher's voice alerted Officer Roy Wilson. Although the streets had been clearing for a couple of hours, it was still a weekend that meant an increase in the number of calls for the police. With Christmas just four days away, city streets had kept the department busier than usual.

"Baker Three, go ahead, Central."

"Respond to The Rex Plaza, 619 North Gloster. A subject was found in the parking lot. Condition is unknown. Emergency crew is in route."

"10-4, Central. I'm on my way." Wilson wiped sweat from his forehead. Being a large man with arthritis in his knees and a hot-nature that only an Alaskan vacation could soothe, it wasn't uncommon to see the officer wiping his forehead from time to time even in the dead of winter.

Wilson slammed his foot against the gas pedal. The tires of his 1973 Chevy Impala screeched as he sped down the highway. Sirens from other patrol cars echoed through the city streets as fellow officers assisted Wilson to the scene. He flew into the parking lot, flinging his car door open and hurriedly walked over to the area where a few bystanders stood watching. The temperature outside was only 33 degrees, but Wilson was pulling his jacket off. The cold air created a fog each time he breathed out of his mouth.

Wilson stood over Devon Bradford. The wounded man was lying face down on the pavement. He nudged him with his foot. Devon could only moan. He was drifting in and out of consciousness. Wilson kneeled beside his body and rolled him over. He looked over Devon and touched his chest. His brown flannel shirt was saturated with blood.

"This man's been shot! Wilson shouted to the other officers who had already arrived and were approaching the scene. Where's that damn ambulance?"

Wilson grabbed his radio. "Central, have you notified the detective division?

"10-4, Baker Three, David 3 is on call. He's on his way."

"10-4. A man has been shot." Wilson was loud, speaking fast and breathless into the microphone.

Seconds later, the flashing red lights from the ambulance could be seen from a short distance along with Detective Bobby Johnson trailing behind in his unmarked patrol unit. Johnson sped into the parking lot. He left his car door open and headed to Wilson's side. His long gray hair was tightly wrapped in a ponytail with a leather shoestring. Dressed in denim and a jacket with a dream catcher emblem on the back, he was known as the renegade in the department. His love for the Native American Indian was exemplified in his appearance. Johnson puffed on his cigarette as he looked around at the crowd that was gathering. By now, a few guests and employees had gathered in the front parking lot of the motel.

Officer Wilson stepped back from the man's body as paramedics pushed past the officers. He towered over the scene, looking like a linebacker for the Dallas Cowboys as he stood nearby watching while the paramedics began to check Devon's motionless body for a pulse.

"We've got a weak pulse on this guy," the paramedic shouted. He noticed the gunshot wounds and began to cut Devon's shirt from his body. His shirt and undershirt were clearly soaked with blood. The bullet holes in the material were precise.

"I'll take that shirt." Johnson stepped forward as the paramedic flung the shirt away from the wounded man's body. He glanced at the detective with irritation.

The emergency crew continued to work frantically to get Devon Bradford on the stretcher. As he watched the paramedics load the man in the ambulance, Johnson overheard one of them say the man had been shot in the chest. Then without warning, a shout came from across the parking lot.

"Liz! Liz has been shot!"

Wilson jerked around to see where the commotion was coming from. His knees cracked and throbbed as he ran to the blue Chevy Impala. He jerked on the driver's side door, but the door was jammed. A huge dent was in the front fender of the driver's side. He went around to the passenger side and shined a flashlight into the car. The still body of a woman hanging over the front seat stunned the officer. A pistol lay on the seat just inches away from her body.

"I need some help over here! We need another ambulance!" Wilson yelled, wiping his forehead. He laid his flashlight on the ground and reached in the car for Liz's arm.

A paramedic ran over to help Wilson pull the body from the car. He immediately noticed the gunshot wounds and placed his fingers on Liz's neck to check for a pulse while fumbling to get his stethoscope on her chest. The gunshot wound to the head had inflicted a perfect round hole behind her left ear.

There was no pulse. Her eyes were slightly open. He carefully placed his fingers on her eyelids and pulled her lids fully open to inspect her pupils. Her eyes had already been set. Her skin appeared pale with traces of blue. He cleared his voice. "She's dead. Probably been dead a good thirty minutes or so."

The paramedic shook his head and backed away. "I'll radio the hospital to send another ambulance." His tone was regretful as he thought of the approaching holidays.

Wilson stood still with his hands on his holster belt while Captain Ray Sullivan who had just arrived moments earlier puffed on his cigarette. He stood at a distance and quietly supervised the scene. He was a quiet man and highly respected by his subordinates. He treated the younger officers like they were his children rather than his employees, always watching out for them and even hosting frequent cookouts for everyone on the shift. He was 6' 3" tall with a strong manly presence and charismatic air. It wasn't uncommon for women to show their appreciation for his rugged good looks. Women flirted incessantly with him.

Sullivan's deep-set dark eyes were fixed on the body of Liz Bradford. He studied the scene for a moment and pondered over the position of Devon Bradford's body and how Liz Bradford had just been discovered. He ran his fingers across his lips, and there was no doubt that he was forming an opinion of what had just happened at The Rex Plaza.

Sullivan flicked his cigarette to the ground and started for the door to the lounge. The heavy wooden door slowly eased shut as he stepped inside the front foyer. The motel housekeepers were busy dusting the ornate frames of the oil paintings hanging in the foyer and cleaning the tile floor. Trickles of water could be heard from the built-in wall fountain beside the hostess's desk. A faint scent of sweet cigars lingered in the air from the dining room. Majestic, ornate buffets and various antique pieces made of cherry wood filled the restaurant. Each piece was hand carved to perfection. Italian style chairs were pushed carefully under the round tables covered with crisp, white linen tablecloths. Inside the dining hall, the hard wood floors were being polished. The windows were covered with folds of rich, burgundy colored velvet trimmed in fringe and tassels. It was a setting for the elite and the romantic at heart.

The last two waitresses in the restaurant were busy setting the tables with spotless goblets and wine stems. Sullivan looked over his head. The brass and glass chandeliers provided just the right amount of light for a romantic experience the motel was famous for. The motel was voted as the "most romantic dining experience in town". It wasn't any wonder that Sullivan had been here several times for domestic disputes. Husbands had come through the back door of the lounge many times only to be met by their wives waiting in the hall. Love and war was famous at The Rex Plaza. It was Tupelo's hot spot, a town of slightly more than 20,000 people where most people knew each other. There was a lot of old money in Tupelo. A person with any clout at all was often courted at The Rex Plaza and showered with attention. And for those married 'wanna be bachelors' that didn't want the trouble that the front door entrance could cause, The Rex Plaza provided a back door entrance/exit.

Elvis Presley had put Tupelo on the map having been born on the East side in a shack. He often spoke fondly of his hometown when he recounted his boyhood days at Shake Rag where the black community welcomed the future King of Rock –n- Roll. He had frequented The Rex Plaza along with Johnny Cash and others who wanted to play some late night poker in Room 105. Although Elvis was not seen in Tupelo very often, his portraits were proudly displayed in the motel's foyer.

Sullivan walked toward the door to the bar and gently eased the door open as it creaked inch by inch. The bartender glanced up at Sullivan as he twisted a rag in a wine glass polishing it to perfection for the next guest. He reached above his head and placed the glass stem in the overhang. The bar was quite large for the small room, the dance floor only wide enough to accommodate about twenty people.

The bartender adjusted the eyeglasses that sat firmly against his nose. His black bow tie hung to the side of his collar. The front of his white shirt still looked freshly pressed except for the sleeves twisted half-way up his arms.

"May I help you?" Ben Johnson's voice was more hoarse than usual. His voice was unforgettable with its soft, raspy tone, and his typical way of looking at someone from a sideways glance made him almost resemble a snapshot from Hollywood's lost archive.

He pushed the sleeves further up his arms as he reached to empty dirty ashtrays lined across the bar top.

He wasn't surprised to see the officer and had wondered if they would come in the lounge to talk to anyone about the incident.

"Yeah, I hope so. Sullivan walked over to the bar and pulled up a barstool. I need to ask you a couple of questions. Maybe you can help me out."

Ben shrugged his shoulders. "Sure."

"The waitress out front—did you know her?"

"Liz? Yes, sir, she worked here." Ben cleared his throat.

"Did you know her husband?"

"No. I recognized him when he came in the restaurant from time to time. He was an odd fellow. Kinda sneaky acting and mean." Ben continued to polish the top of the bar then stopped and looked Sullivan dead in the face.

Sullivan stared back. "How so?"

Ben propped his hands on the counter and looked at the ceiling studying the tiles of pressed tin. "Liz told us about him beating her. She mentioned that he was real jealous. He came in tonight looking for her." Ben paused and studied Sullivan.

"Did you talk to him?"

"Yeah, he just asked me if I knew where she was, and I told him no. You know, she always seemed scared of him." Ben shook his head with sympathy for Liz.

Sullivan wrote in a small spiral notebook. "What did he do then?"

"He just turned around and left. I didn't see him again. Then, my step dad came running in an hour later saying that a man was lying in the parking lot." Ben pointed toward the door. He shook his head again with remorse. "I sure do hate this happened. Poor Liz. She was a sweet lady. Never gave us a minute's trouble."

"How long had she worked here?"

"Just a few months."

Sullivan flipped the notebook shut. "Thanks. If you think of anything else, here's my card." He turned and walked out the door. He adjusted his gun holster as he stood staring down the well-lit city street. His next stop must be North Mississippi Medical Center, the city's only hospital and the region's closest major medical center.

✝

CHAPTER 4

It was approximately 1:15 a.m., and Devon Bradford lay quiet as Natalie Houston pushed the stretcher down the long corridor. His moaning and grunting had ceased as he fell into a light sleep. She glanced down at her patient and allowed her eyes to roam the length of his body. She noticed his nose, a bit large for his face. He reminded her of an Indian man she once knew, tall and dark with a distinguished nose. His thick hair was coal black with traces of gray, and his shirt had been cut off him to reveal a stunning manly chest, thick with hair the same color as his head. His olive toned skin was smooth and dark as if he had just spent a few hours in the sunshine. Natalie took a deep breath as she admired all she had been noticing. Dark men had always been her weakness, even the ones not worth getting to know.

The doors to the operating room swung open. "What we got here, girls?" Dr. Jay Adams asked as he hurriedly walked around the gurney. The thoracic surgeon had already been in the hospital when the ambulance arrived. He was a short, stocky man with graying hair and a cocky, aristocratic attitude. He thought most people weren't as smart as he was. He was known about the hospital for being volatile and untrustworthy as a friend. And if he didn't like someone as a co-worker, they had better be prepared for the sabotage he could create in their career. But, if there was anything worth respecting about Dr. Jay Adams, it was his dedication to his job and his determination to save lives. He and Natalie had that in common.

"He's been shot in the chest, Dr. Adams. I was downstairs when they brought him in." Natalie watched as the doctor bent over the quiet body of Devon Bradford.

Dr. Adams lightly touched the area surrounding the three bullet holes. The wounds were small, but precise. He placed the strips of gauze back in place until the techs got ready to shave his chest.

Dr. Adams grumbled under his breath. "Looks like this is going to take a few hours." He turned and looked at Natalie who stood near the corner of the room with her hands clasped together. She looked toward the floor while waiting for his instruction.

"How much coffee you had, Ms. Houston?"

"Enough", she said frowning. "Enough. In fact, I was on my coffee break when they brought him in." She ran her fingers over her surgery cap in search of a free strand of her shoulder length brown hair. She felt uneasy around Dr. Adams and tried to avoid him as much as she could. She had heard about his reputation and didn't care to be his next victim.

"You know what happened to this guy?" Dr. Adams began to scrub his hands.

"I was told he was shot at The Rex Plaza."

Dr. Adams laughed to himself. He looked up and mockingly replied. "Well, I'd say you're certainly on top of things, Nurse Houston. It's obvious he was shot. What else can you tell us?"

Natalie's face turned red. She wanted to tell him to go to hell, but he was the doctor, the boss, and some battles weren't worth fighting when it came to risking her job.

She hesitated. "I- I really don't know anything else. Sorry."

Dr. Adams ignored her and walked around the table. Natalie followed, getting into position for surgery. Even after years as a nurse, she still couldn't get over the initial shock of the knife in the operating room. The thought of her patient dying bothered her. On several occasions, she had left the hospital only to have dreams of her patients. She never considered that the dead were trying to thank her. She didn't believe in ghosts. If there was a spiritual world, the souls of the deceased had to be either in heaven or hell. There couldn't be any other place. At least, that's what she had been taught in the small Southern Baptist churches she had always attended. Her brother was a Baptist minister, and if he didn't know the Truth, no one did.

Five hours passed. Natalie Houston stood over Devon Bradford. She focused her eyes on her patient and watched as Dr. Adams removed the three bullets from Devon Bradford's chest. With an unmatched skill, Dr. Adams removed the last bullet and dropped it in the metal tray that Natalie held. The metal reacted like a bell ringing as each bullet had dropped against the flat, stainless steel plate. The clinking seemed loud in the room almost creating an echo. Minutes seemed to pass like hours as Dr. Adams closed Devon's chest. The surgery had been a success. Devon's wounds had not been critical. His vital signs were satisfactory, but he had lost a lot of blood. He would have to be transferred to intensive care for at least 24 hours.

Natalie took a deep breath. Her eyes had become heavy, and her feet were aching. She smiled to herself. She had assisted in saving another life. It felt good. She paused to study her patient and wondered what had led to his being shot. She wondered who he was. Not his name, but who was the man asleep on the table in front of her? Had he been a victim? She quickly brushed off her thoughts. There had been many times she had wondered things about her patients, but it wasn't her business to know her patient's personal affairs. Her responsibility was saving lives.

Dr. Adams sighed heavily and began to yank off his gloves as he made his way to the door. Natalie felt her shoulders relax as she followed behind the doctor. Her upper back ached from being bent over the operating table. She still suffered her own agony with a slipped disc from a couple of years ago. Her back had never been the same since the injury. She was tired and fatigued that day, and she didn't realize the weight of the old man she was bathing when she pulled him from the tub. It happened quickly, and it cost her six weeks off work recuperating from back surgery.

Natalie stretched her hands over her head. She pulled off her surgical gloves and turned on the hot water in the large stainless steel sink. She scrubbed her hands vigorously as her mind drifted back to the patient on the table. A mixture of emotions suddenly swept over her. Grief. Confusion. Attraction. She was bewildered. It was as if she was being manipulated by something outside herself. Feeling things that were not her own. Natalie let out a sigh. She summed up the strange new awareness to long hours and tired feet. A long hot bath would do her well. And sleep. Yes, she needed sleep.

But, she should have listened to what she couldn't hear. She should have been aware of that heightened thing called instinct. Instead, she was blindfolded by her own incognizance. She was walking steadfast into a treacherous future being revealed before her very eyes.

CHAPTER 5

It was early Christmas Eve morning. While Devon Bradford lay quiet in his hospital room bed, the family and friends of Liz Bradford gathered at the church just down the highway from the mansion that once belonged to Liz Bradford. Lindenwood had been hers, built with the children in mind. It was her dream home, and all she had ever wanted other than a love she had not found. The Bradford children reluctantly prepared for their mother's funeral. James Bradford put on his finest shirt and tie not sure that it matched. The eighteen-year old son had the sole responsibility of getting his three other sisters to the funeral on time. Rebecca finished brushing her hair and left her room to check on Susan and Audrey, her two younger sisters. They were all just three years apart with Rebecca recently turning fourteen. As the sisters walked to the front door of the house, the door swung open with a gust of wind. The girls jumped. A force of wind swept across their faces, bitter cold and dry. Rebecca rushed to shut the door. A mournful howling could be heard as the wind swept through the upstairs of the mansion across the banister and out the upstairs balcony.

"What was that?" Rebecca yelled across the room. Audrey and Susan shrugged their shoulders and pulled their jackets tighter across their chests.

Rebecca shivered. "We better get going. James is probably waiting for us outside." The wind's howl had unnerved her with its distinct cry.

Rebecca slammed the door behind them. They crossed the front yard and got into James's 1965 Mustang. "What took you so long?" His voice was agitated.

"Nothing. Just drive." Rebecca shot back.

The drive was short, across the highway and up the hill. The small church held the body of Liz Bradford and the several family members and friends that had gathered to say goodbye. Liz's grave had been dug the day before. Her body was to be buried beside her deceased daughter, Caroline Bradford. The fourteen-year-old girl had drowned the year before.

As James parked the Mustang, Audrey sat staring out the window at the graveyard across from the church. Her face reflected a somber frown in the pane of glass, her dark brown hair and eyes a living reflection of their mother's features.

She chewed on her finger as she studied the mound of dirt that had been poured for her mother's grave. Her sister's grave still had bare spots where the grass had not grown back. She remembered the familiar green tent that stood over the gravesite. The graves were at the far side of the graveyard and could be seen from the upstairs bay window at Lindenwood. Tears of longing and grief swept over Audrey.

"Audrey, let's go." Rebecca nudged Audrey in the arm. Audrey opened the door of the car and slid off the seat. Her grandmother was waiting for her on the front steps of the church.

Moments later, the Bradford children escorted by Liz's mother entered the church where their mother lay resting among mounds of funeral wreaths. The fresh flowers emitted a strong sweet odor throughout the parlor and brightened the softly lit scene with blues, pinks, and blues. A few red and ivory poinsettias were placed near the casket casting a dreadful memory of Christmas for the children. Mourners lined the hallway waiting to pay their last respects to the deceased mother of six children, a daughter and wife, and a hairdresser for many in the community who came to see Liz when she wasn't working at The Rex Plaza.

The soft murmurs of people's chatter filled the church parlor. There was an eerie unease in the air as several visitors whispered. Questions filled the minds of those closest to Liz and Devon Bradford. Had Devon killed her? Did he catch her with another man? Was there any way that Liz could have realistically left her husband without suffering this type of demise? Everyone seemed to have their own opinions about what had happened. The rumors were already circulating around the community. Some believed that Devon had killed Liz and then shot himself. Others believed that someone else had shot Devon Bradford after he killed Liz. Everyone had a theory, but the people who knew the truth were either not talking or dead. Audrey made her way to the casket. Her face mirrored the horror and grief of a newly orphaned child. Thoughts raced through her mind. Tomorrow was Christmas. It would not be worth remembering but would become a part of her for the remainder of her life. She stood quiet with her hands clasped. Tears flooded her eyes. Her mother was gone, and her dad was now absent resting in a hospital bed while she and four other children watched as their mother was lowered into the earth. What would happen to her without her mother? Audrey studied her mother. The reality of death frightened her. She wondered how scared her mom must have been when she died.

Liz's body had been carefully prepared. Her make-up was heavy with her lips having been painted a crimson red, but the dark rouge Liz Bradford always wore was absent this morning. Her hair was combed neat and sprayed stiff with hairspray against her head, unlike the way Liz fixed it herself in her own shop at Lindenwood. The children had selected a light blue dress to cover her tall full frame. Although her thick dark hair had been styled to cover the bullet wound, the perfect round hole behind her left ear had inflicted an exit wound on the opposite side of the temple. The burns and bruises on her skin could still be easily detected. As Audrey examined her mother's lifeless figure, she reached out to touch her mother's hand. It wasn't the same hand she remembered. Her hands were cold now and hard. And her mouth had been sewn shut in a dull, expressionless manner. Liz Bradford's lips were silent, but little did anyone know the quiet Liz Bradford would soon be making a grand entrance right back in the Lindenwood mansion where she belonged.

✝

CHAPTER 6

Two days after Christmas, Sullivan made plans to see Devon Bradford. The morning drive with Chief Clayton was quiet as the captain thought about the past week's events pertaining to the Bradford shooting. He hoped he would get some answers from Devon Bradford. Police had been informed that he had been moved from the Intensive Care Unit into a regular hospital room.

Sullivan's face revealed his lack of sleep from the past three nights. His eyes were traced with dark circles and his skin looked dry from the toll of winter weather. Working extra security jobs left little time for sleep. He wheeled the car into a nearby parking space at the entrance to the ER. Chief Clayton stepped out of the car. Clayton was a hard-nosed man of forty years with salt and pepper hair. He wore square framed glasses he depended on to see two feet in front of him, but he was well respected by his subordinates for his knowledge and skill as a law officer.

"Ray, have you talked to any of the family yet?"

"Yeah, just one of his daughters though. She claims Mr. Bradford drove to Tupelo around 10:00 pm to trade vehicles with her mother."

"Well, let's see what he's got to say." The captain and chief walked through the sliding glass doors and proceeded down the long hall. The smell of hospital disinfectants tickled Sullivan's nose. He pinched his nose shut and rubbed his watery eyes.

Two floors up, Devon Bradford lay still in his hospital room bed. His chest was still bandaged from the surgery a few days ago. He looked around the room and stared at the ceiling. He knew it would only be a matter of time before the police would question him. The last few days had been a blur since Mrs. Victor from The Rex Plaza had paid him a visit to inform him of Liz's death. He knew he must be very careful of his words and actions until the police went away. He had survived. Now everyone would be expecting answers from him.

A knock at the door startled Devon. "Come in." His voice was weak.

Sullivan pushed the door open and walked toward Devon's bed.

"Mornin, Mr. Bradford. I'm Captain Ray Sullivan with the Tupelo Police Department and this is Chief Robert Clayton. We're here to ask you a few questions about the shooting at The Rex Plaza last Saturday night." Devon looked wide-eyed at the two men entering his room. Sullivan made himself at home taking a seat next to Devon's bed.

"Well, I really don't remember much." Devon's voice was barely above a whisper.

"Can you tell us what you do remember?" Chief Clayton persisted.

"Uh, yes, Sir. I remember getting shot. I'll tell you that. My wife shot me. I wrestled with her over the gun, and I remember having my hands on the barrel."

"What were you doing at The Rex Plaza last Saturday night?" Sullivan sat quiet and observant of Devon's body language as Clayton continued to drill him.

Devon cleared his voice and began to tug at his bed sheets. "My wife and I had an argument the night before. She left the next morning and told me to bring the Chevy Impala to her at work later that night. It hadn't been running right, and I worked on it all day to get it running."

Devon rubbed his chest bandage. "I feel pretty bad- if you guys don't mind coming back another time." Devon started to feel uneasy. If he said the wrong thing, he could find himself in jail.

"Certainly not, Mr. Bradford. Chief Clayton turned to walk out the door. But, when you get out of the hospital, I need for you to come down to the station and talk to me. We need to get a statement from you."

"Okay. Devon nodded in agreement. I'll phone you as soon as I'm released." He faked a friendly smile.

Sullivan nodded in agreement, his cool blue eyes fixed on Devon Bradford.

"We'll expect to hear from you in a few days. Appreciate your time." Clayton turned to follow Sullivan out. Sullivan chewed his bottom lip as he contemplated the case. What was Devon Bradford's motive for killing his wife? He said they had an argument the night before. Did he plan the death of Liz Bradford? Sullivan had seen this before, a typical crime of passion. Domestic disputes were common to turn deadly, but this investigation would take more than a few days to close. Their only witness was now buried six feet under.

"Sullivan, you know I'm going to be out of town for the next three months." Clayton said as a matter of fact. Sullivan glanced sideways at Clayton with raised eyebrows.

"Yes, sir. So, who's in charge of this case?"

Clayton grinned and slapped Sullivan on the shoulder. "You are."

The following day Sullivan found himself sitting behind his desk mulling over his new responsibility. With Clayton gone to the National FBI academy, Sullivan knew he had more work than he could handle. He reached for the folder labeled "Bradford case". He began to review the evidence that was collected from the crime scene. Several bullet hulls and a smear of dried blood had been taken from the Chevy Impala, but his lack of witnesses made it impossible for him to determine what crime had been committed. He picked up the phone and dialed Devon Bradford's home. The phone rang several times before anyone answered.

"Hello?"

"Hello, who's speaking, please?"

"Uh- this is James Bradford."

"James, this is Captain Ray Sullivan with the Tupelo Police Department. I'm investigating the shooting of Devon and Liz Bradford. Are you a relative of theirs?"

"Yes, sir. I'm their son." James stated as a matter-of- fact.

"Good. I would really like to ask you a few questions about the night before the shooting. Can you come by the station this afternoon?" Sullivan knew he would probably say no and that would give him an opportunity to go to Lindenwood for a look around.

"Well, uh-

"How 'bout I meet you at your house. It won't take long." Sullivan persisted.

"I guess that'll be okay." Even though James felt a sense of obligation, he wasn't quite sure how to dodge Sullivan.

Sullivan looked at the clock. "I'll see you in forty-five minutes." The captain grabbed his notebook and rushed out the door.

At 1:00 pm, Sullivan pulled into the gravel driveway at Lindenwood. The stately Colonial style home set several feet from the highway on a large tree covered lot. The exterior of the mansion was built with red brick. Three, grand white columns supported the front porch of the two-story house.

As he shifted the car in park, he noticed a young man walking on a balcony directly above the garage. He wore only a faded pair of jeans, and his lean muscular frame revealed a laborer's physique.

Sullivan walked to the front door looking all around as he went. As he raised his hand to knock, the door opened. Loud music came flooding out the door.

James was surprised. "Oh, hey, man. Let me turn this music down. Come on in."

James's shaggy light-brown hair was still damp from the shower. His jaw was strong and his eyes a piercing blue. Sullivan watched as James disappeared through a door leading off the great room. James walked with an air of arrogance, his chest pushed forward. Sullivan looked up the stairs. Several bedrooms and a kitchen were on the second floor. The house had a peculiar sweet smell like burning incense. Sullivan sniffed the air trying to decipher the odor. He wondered if the incense was being used to mask the stench of burning marijuana. Sullivan re-focused his attention to James as he re-entered the room.

"How can I help, Sir?" James was friendly and his tone almost inquisitive as if there was some surprise about Sullivan's inquiry.

Sullivan thought James seemed too eager under the circumstances. Did he know who shot and killed his mother? Wasn't he aware that his father would be a prime suspect?

Sullivan made himself at home and took a seat on a black leather sofa that sat just outside the master suite.

"Why don't we sit down?" He opened a notebook and began to scribble the date.

"James, were you home the Friday night before the shooting?"

"Yes, sir, I was."

"Can you tell me the nature of the argument Mr. and Mrs. Bradford were having?"

"No, not really. I was in the other room. I just heard some hollering."

"Do you know what they were arguing about?"

"No, I don't. They hadn't been getting along for several months though and sometimes they fought."

"Were there any physical blows exchanged between them?" Sullivan frowned at James's lack of specifics. He wasn't providing much information.

"Just hair-pulling."

"Were you here the morning your mother left?"

"No, I went deer hunting."

"What time was that?"

James let out a sigh and rubbed his head. "Bout' 5:30 that mornin."

"Okay, I appreciate your time. Sullivan reluctantly shut his notebook. If you have anything you'd like to talk to me about, here's my card." Sullivan stood up to leave and began to step toward the door.

"Sir, there is one other thing I just thought of." James rubbed his hands together and shoved them in his pockets. "The night Daddy and Mama were fighting, I did hear *her* threaten his life."

✟

CHAPTER 7

It was the day after New Year's. Rose Smith's modest apartment was silent, surrounded by a blind darkness. The hall nightlight had gone out when the electricity suddenly flickered off. She lay in bed finally drifting off to sleep after numerous hours of insomnia. She could not get over seeing her best friend and co-worker dead in the parking lot of The Rex Plaza just days before. Liz had been afraid of Devon Bradford, but she didn't think he was capable of murder. Rose pulled the blankets around her face, unaware that the temperature in her apartment was steadily dropping. Rose began to drift into a light sleep. She grunted and twisted in the bed. Her eyes twitched, and she whimpered while fading in and out of lucidity. She saw the face of Liz Bradford. Her hands were outstretched, her eyes filled with despair as she pleaded for help. She spat blood with each word she spoke.

"Rose, help me! Devon is going to kill me! You have to help me! Please!" she cried.

Blood trickled down her throat and seeped from the wound in her back. Her face was pale white except for the burst vessels in her skin. She stepped closer toward Rose until she was able to reach out and grab her arm.

Rose Smith jerked awake. She breathed heavy, her breath creating a chilling fog. The bed sheets were damp with sweat. This was the fifth time she had dreamt of Liz Bradford. She rubbed her arm where Liz Bradford's hand had been. She threw her legs over the side of the bed and sat up combing her fingers through her short, brown hair. The vision of Liz's head with bald spots and the bruises about her neck continued to bother her, and her waking hours were filled with thoughts of her conversation with Liz the day she died.

She looked around the room. She sniffed the air and detected an odor of perfume. She knew she had not sprayed anything before she went to bed. Her eyes were heavy and her head ached from lack of sleep. She thought about the hours before the murder. She remembered Liz bringing her clothes over to her house the day she died. Rose rubbed her face. She felt an unnerving presence in the room. She looked all around her finding nothing to satisfy her unease.

Was Liz Bradford trying to communicate with her and if so, *why?* Rose slid off the bed and stepped into the small bathroom next to her bed. She opened the medicine cabinet door and reached for a sleeping aid she had bought a couple of days before. She tossed the pill to the back of her throat and closed her eyes as she drank from a small, plastic cup. She climbed back in bed and was relieved when the bedside lamp came back on. She left it burning and closed her eyes.

Three weeks had passed before Sullivan heard anything out of Devon Bradford until he showed up at the Police Department intent on picking up his wife's Chevy Impala. He entered the front door of the PD wearing a neatly pressed pair of black pants and wingtip shoes. His shirt was oxford white and neatly pressed. He was there to see Captain Sullivan. The dispatcher motioned for Devon to come through the lobby doors where Sullivan was waiting to see him.

"Hello, Mr. Bradford." Sullivan studied Devon's demeanor.

Devon offered a friendly smile. He was confident that his visit to the police department would be over soon. They had nothing on him. There were no witnesses. He had nothing to fear.

"I'm here to pick up my wife's car and any belongings of mine y'all have." Devon extended a handshake to Sullivan as if he were campaigning for office. Sullivan ignored his gesture.

"Mr. Bradford, I'm afraid I'm not going to be able to let you take the car." Sullivan frowned, his face locked with determination.

"Why not?" Devon's smile dropped from his face. Sullivan pulled a pair of handcuffs from his side and reached for Devon's wrist. He looked at Sullivan with disbelief.

"Mr. Bradford, I am placing you under arrest for the murder of Liz Bradford. You have the right to remain silent. Anything you say can and will be used against you in a court of law. You have the right to an attorney. If you cannot afford an attorney, one will be appointed for you. You may stop answering questions at any time you decide to exercise these rights. Do you understand?" Sullivan stared at Devon.

"Yes." Devon let out a sigh. He sat down in a chair nearby and rubbed the palm of his hand. A rush of anxiety filled Devon's core. Thousands of thoughts flooded his mind. Job loss. Money loss. More money loss. Devon Bradford always knew to the penny how much he was worth, and he couldn't stand the thought of being locked up, not able to control his cash flow. Too many people depended on him.

"Mr. Bradford, would you like to give me your statement at this time?" Sullivan signaled for a witness to come in the office.

"Yeah, I guess so." Devon cleared his voice and thought about what he was going to say.

"Okay, Mr. Bradford, tell me what happened on December 21, 1974." Sullivan reached for his notebook. He sat on the corner of the desk with his feet propped on the side of a chair, pen in hand.

"My wife and I had had a big fight the night before. We were just having some family problems. The next morning my wife got up and started piling clothes in the truck. She said she was leaving and for me to bring the car to her work later that night and we would trade vehicles since all my work tools were on the truck. The car hadn't been running properly. Then, I worked on the car and later in the afternoon, I took my daughter Susan, Christmas shopping in Tupelo. We saw the truck in downtown Tupelo, and I knew Liz was not at work. So, I went back home and took a nap. I had been sick with a cold for several days and wasn't feeling well." Devon paused and looked at Sullivan. He waited for Sullivan to say something, but he continued to scribble on a notebook.

"Later that night, the kids came in and woke me up and told me to go get the truck. I left around 10:00 p.m. and drove slow since the car hadn't been running well. I got to The Rex Plaza and found my wife in the motel lobby. We walked outside and began to talk a little while she unloaded her clothes from the truck. She asked if I wanted to go have a cup of coffee, and I said okay. But then the Pancake house down the street was too busy, and I said I wanted to go home. We got back to the motel and were fussing a little. I don't remember anything after we got back to the motel."

Devon's brows began to furrow as he studied the ground.

"What time did you get back to The Rex Plaza?" Sullivan pressed for more answers. Devon flinched. "I don't know. I really don't remember anything else. I don't want to talk anymore."

Sullivan leaned away from Devon. "Okay, are you telling me that you wish to exercise your rights at this time?"

"Yes, that's right." Devon realized they were going to pin the death of his wife on him. His hands begin to tremble.

"Please empty all your pockets, Mr. Bradford, and put your belongings in this envelope." Sullivan took the envelope and patted Devon down.

"Walk this way." Sullivan escorted Devon to a jail cell.

"I'll be back shortly for you." He had no expression on his face as he slammed the steel doors shut.

Devon stood staring at the wall and grumbled under his breath. He thought about Liz Bradford. This was all her fault. The sleazy whore had been cheating on him. She deserved what she got for making a fool out of him. There was no way he was going to serve a day in jail because of her. He needed an attorney, a good attorney. He sat down on a squeaky cot and waited.

Three hours later, Devon walked through the doors of his Lindenwood home. He stood in the great room and looked all around the top floor of the house. He reminisced of a time when he and Liz were building the house. Liz had been excited about having plenty of room. He admired the velvet-trimmed wallpaper Liz had custom ordered for the downstairs living area. The red carpet accented the black leather furniture she furnished the house with. Now all this would be his alone. He felt a sense of emptiness, but didn't miss Liz Bradford as much as he missed the presence of someone to manipulate and control. He simply had too much going on in his life to take on the role of father and mother to the four children still living at Lindenwood.

The house had an eerie silence as he walked to the door of his bedroom. A heavy aura seemed to float in the air of the master suite as Devon entered the room. He walked to the edge of the bed and sat down. He leaned back against the pillows and closed his eyes. Just as he took a deep breath and began to settle himself for a nap, his eyes flew open. He thought he had heard someone's feet sliding across the carpet. He propped himself up on his elbows and looked about the room, but no one was there. Still, he felt someone or something lurking closer toward him.

"Who's there?" Devon demanded.

Liz Bradford moved slowly around the room, invisible to the human eye but very real in her presence. With a sudden fury, a picture of Devon and Liz Bradford crashed to the floor. Devon swung around only to see an empty room. The hair on the back of his neck began to rise. He could have sworn he heard laughter over his shoulder. What was happening to him? He turned around and looked all about the room. Nothing was out of place. But, in the corner of the bedroom resting across Liz's chaise lounge was her favorite leopard print coat. She had been wearing the jacket the night she died. Devon froze. Suddenly, it felt as if she were still very much alive.

Devon grunted as he felt a chill settling over him. He quickly turned to walk out of the room headed for the upstairs kitchen. He needed a glass of whiskey, something to calm him.

He looked puzzled as he walked over to examine the front door. Devon paused with a curious look on his face. He rubbed the side of his face, chills creeping up his back. Who could have opened the door? He tried to brush the unsettling feeling aside. Stress and worry were causing him to hear voices. It was the only logical explanation. His life had been turned upside down in just a few minutes, and if he were found guilty of killing his wife, he knew he might spend the rest of his life in jail. What would happen to Lindenwood and his money?

He was fortunate that Moore Distribution had supported him after Liz's death. Rumors had already circulated the community, but Devon had successfully won most everyone's sympathy. He was a charming, likable fellow. He had an instant charisma that few people could resist. His power was magical. Like a vampire, he could charm and hypnotize the most resilient character. He made sure everyone knew that he was only defending his life against a cheating wife. Devon sipped on a glass of whiskey. He cleared his throat and propped his elbows on the snack bar in the upstairs kitchen. Questions roamed through his mind searching for a place to stop and find answers. Who would take care of his children if he were found guilty? If there was anything Devon Bradford did care about, it was his children. They were born of his seed, precious and sacred like his money. He was stingy with money and his children. Nothing else was really important as long as he didn't have to choose between the loss of his children and his obsession with money.

Devon rubbed his face, staring at the wall across from the kitchen bar. He knew he would have to call a family meeting over dinner. It was imperative that the Bradford children be coached about their behavior and their story on the night of December 21st. His fate could rest in one of their hands. He knew there were no witnesses to the crime at The Rex Plaza, but he also knew what the police were thinking. And the grand jury would be meeting in eight days to decide if he went to trial.

✝

CHAPTER 8

Devon Bradford stood before the grand jury. Judge Frank Whit shuffled some papers as he looked over the rim of his glasses. His dark hair was seasoned with gray and pressed firmly against his head. He seemed much bigger than his 5' 9" frame under his dark cloak. He was a popular guy in the community. His gift of gab made him many friends but sometimes drove others crazy. He could convince a PhD that he knew more than they did. Although he might not be an authority on the subject at hand, he could fool anyone if they had plenty of time to listen. The judge cleared his throat as he prepared to read the jury's conclusion.

"Will the defendant please rise?" Devon Bradford slowly stood with his hands clasped behind his back. "Mr. Bradford, after reviewing the evidence in this case, it is the decision of the court to try this case on the charge of murder. How do you plead?" The judge looked stern.

"Not guilty, your honor," Devon stated loudly. He hadn't spoken that loudly in his entire life. He never spoke much louder than a whisper, but today he wanted to make sure everyone heard him since all his family as well as Liz's was in the courthouse.

Attorney Bill Russell shook his head. "Don't worry, Mr. Bradford. This is a closed case as far as you're concerned." Russell patted Devon on the back. He pulled his pants up over his bulging stomach, and took a drag off the cigarette hanging out of the corner of his mouth. Ashes fell off the end of the butt. He quickly flicked them off the table.

Russell always had a problem keeping his pants pulled up, his weight being the real irritation. He smoked with a fever, refusing to let his lungs rest more than a few minutes. His clothes were saturated with smoke. He tried to drown out the tobacco smell every morning by soaking his neck with Aramis cologne. Although his appearance looked disheveled on occasion, he was a damn good lawyer in the courtroom, relentless when it came to arguments. Nothing intimidated the attorney except a boring case. He was a devoted husband to his wife, Betty. She was the one thing in his life that had been constant and true. For every battle he had fought, she had been the chorus singing him to victory.

"Well, Mr. Russell, if it's not a closed case, then I expect you will do whatever it takes to make me a free man." Devon Bradford almost glared at his attorney. He rubbed his hands together as if he were handling a wad of one hundred dollar bills.

Russell cleared his voice and nodded. "I agreed to take this case, didn't I? I've won a lot more than I've lost, Mr. Bradford." He gathered his notes off the defendant's table. He watched Devon.

"Yes, sir, I know. And you must know how troubled I am." Devon felt a need to backtrack. He couldn't afford to piss him off, but he couldn't afford for his attorney to become complacent either.

"Absolutely." Russell's tone was firm. He knew what he must do next.

" Listen, the first thing I need to do is interview all of the children. We need to get our stories straight and our instructions right before anybody goes into that courtroom."

Judge Whitt scribbled on a piece of paper while Devon Bradford sat holding a pack of Winston's. He massaged the cigarette pack anxious to get outside and taste the tobacco that lingered beneath his nose. Although smoking was allowed in the courtroom, it wasn't deemed appropriate for him to smoke. Russell didn't want him to look defiant by any means.

Judge Whitt looked up from his papers. "I'm going to set the bond in this case at $25,000. Court is dismissed." Devon looked over at Russell who was shaking his head in an effort to soothe Devon. "I know what you're thinking. Yeah, it seems a little high, but it doesn't matter. This will be over soon."

"How soon? My damn wife tried to kill me, and I'm going to stand trial for defending myself." Devon's face was screwed up in a look of hate and revenge. He wanted freedom now. Waiting a possible six months before his trial was too long.

Russell nodded. "I know, I know. But, not to lie to you, it might just be six months. Do you have bail money?"

"Oh, yeah. I'm not worried about that." Devon adjusted the waist of his pants with arrogance.

"Good, then. Just go about your life as you normally would or as best you can until we know further. You're a free man, Mr. Bradford. Until you're found guilty in a court of law, you are free."

Devon let out a long sigh. He reached out and shook Russell's hand gripping it tight. "Thanks. When will I hear from you?"

"Soon." Russell picked up his briefcase and walked to the courtroom door. The bailiff escorted Devon out of the courtroom and into the hall where his family was waiting.

The bailiff stopped as one of Devon's brothers stepped forward and put his arms around him. "Everything's going to work out. Don't worry. You have too many of the right people on your side." He spoke low, barely above a mumble.

Devon touched his brother's forearm pulling him closer. He whispered close to his brother's ear. "Listen, I need your help. I don't know how long this is going to take. Can you keep an eye on my children?"

"Yeah, whatever you need, brother."

Devon nodded once. He patted his brother's shoulder and walked out the courtroom doors.

✝

CHAPTER 9

June of 1975 came quicker than Devon Bradford would have liked. It was now time for a jury to decide his fate. Bill Russell had charged him a hefty price for his retainer, but he had promised him freedom. Devon would have paid thousands to stay out of jail. His life was priceless even if he didn't hold his deceased wife in the same regard.

Russell instructed the Bradford children to remain as calm as they could in the courtroom and encouraged them to show grief. All of the children seemed to be cooperative, but they also seemed confused. The girls were still grieving over the loss of their mother, and if anybody poised a problem in their testimony, it would be one of them and not James. James was devoted to his father. Russell had instructed them not to lie, but not to give too much information either. They were only to answer the questions with as little detail as possible. By sticking to yes/no answers, they would have a lesser chance of getting confused. Russell also had cautioned them about their body language and had told Devon Bradford to remain gentleman like in his mannerisms at all times. The jury would be watching, and his demeanor in court could influence their opinions.

The Lee County Courthouse was situated on a low hill in the center of the city. The top of the building resembled a church tower with a clock. The huge clock had kept time since its construction in 1905. It wasn't the first courthouse to stand in its current location. Two other structures had stood there beginning in 1871 just a year after Tupelo had been incorporated in 1870. The final majestic landmark had been erected after two fires had destroyed its previous buildings. Its past held a rich history filled with stories of Civil War days, Nathan Bedford Forrest, and public hangings.

The grounds were plush with rich, green grass. Azaleas painted the landscape with white, pink, and red blooms. Each cluster of bushes had been carefully placed, circling the Magnolia trees scattered around the courthouse lawn. The hedge bushes were neatly trimmed, and garbage bins were placed on all four corners of the lawn to discourage any littering. Inside the courtroom, window size fans hummed steadily as their blades turned with a fervor trying to cool the heated courtroom. Ashtrays were placed in various locations throughout the room. The benches were old and had scribbles of ink in the seats. The smell of the room was characteristic of a time past. The lingering scent of cigars and sweet tobacco still filled the old building.

Devon Bradford sat solemn as he waited for his first day in court. Bill Russell busied himself with his notes on the case while the district attorney, George Dennis and the county prosecutor, Richard Oliver whispered to one another. Oliver, a local attorney and avid historian had spent hour after hour in the courtroom. Prior to taking the role of county prosecutor, he had been one of Tupelo's most sought after criminal defense attorneys. He knew the ins and outs of the courtroom like the back of his hand, and he had an eye for detail. He also knew Bill Russell, and that meant he better be ready to match wits. Although Dennis could handle the courtroom drama, it would be up to Oliver to make sure the prosecution had the facts straight.

"All rise for the Honorable Judge Frank Whit as the Lee County Circuit Court is now in session." The slender, balding bailiff stood aside. His hand rested on his holster as the judge entered the courtroom.

The short, petite court reporter positioned her fingers on the typewriter ready to begin recording the day's testimony. The forty-something year old blond was well known in the county having been born and raised in Tupelo. She had seen her share of murder cases tried in the old court building. She had built her reputation on her attention to detail. There wasn't a testimony given that she didn't record every single syllable that came from a witness's mouth.

Judge Whit scanned the room. "Mornin, you may be seated."

The courtroom was noisy as people took their seats. The family and friends of Devon and Liz Bradford filled the first three benches on both sides of the room.

"Are you ready to call your first witness, Mr. Dennis?" Judge Whit asked as he rubbed the sweat from his brow.

"Yes, sir." George Dennis spoke in a perfect southern drawl. He had the unmistaken character and poise of a southern gentleman. He stood just above average height at 5'10" tall and weighed more than 185 pounds. His mere presence commanded respect even without the deep authoritative voice that rolled from his mouth. With his jet, black hair and hazel eyes he was the picture of masculine Southern charm, a Rhett Butler, and he had all the finesse necessary to carry it off.

"The state calls James Bradford to the stand."

James Bradford approached the bench as if he had done it all his life. He listened intently to the bailiff as he was being sworn in, his eyes glued on the Bible. "Please state your full name and age for the court."

"James Bradford. I'm eighteen years old."

"Mr. Bradford, do you know this man in the courtroom today?" The D.A. motioned to the defendant's table where Devon sat studying his hands.

"Yes, sir. He is my father." James looked in the direction of Devon Bradford.

"And where have you been living, James?"

"At home with my father."

"Did you live at Lindenwood prior to your mother's death?"

"Yes, I did."

"So, you were living at Lindenwood on December 20, 1974?"

"Yes."

Dennis cleared his voice. "That Friday night during the fight between your mother and father, when did you see Devon strike your mother?"

"I object, your honor." Bill Russell jumped to his feet. He pulled his navy blue trousers high on his waist.

"Sustained. Rephrase the question. We haven't established the fact of a fight taking place in the home, Mr. Dennis." Judge Whit cut his eyes at the D.A.

"James, were you at home Friday, December 20, 1974?" Dennis noticed the judge's stare.

"Yes, I was."

"And did you notice anything unusual going on at home that night?"

"No, not really."

"Were your parents both at home that night?"

"Yes."

"What were they doing?"

"They were fussing a little."

"Did you hear any threats of a physical nature?"

"Yes."

"Who made those threats?"

"My mother."

"Where were you in the house during the fight?"

"I was in my bedroom."

"And where were Mr. and Mrs. Bradford?" The D. A. rubbed his finger over his lips as he concentrated on his line of questioning.

"In their bedroom."

"Is that located a far distance from your room?"

"No, sir."

"I have no further questions at this time, your honor." The D.A. took his seat and began to jot notes on a torn piece of paper sticking out of his folder.

"Mr. Russell, do you have any questions for this witness?" Judge Whit asked.

"Yes, your honor." Attorney Bill Russell walked from behind the table twirling a pencil between his fingers.

"James, did you talk to Captain Ray Sullivan at any time before this trial?"

"No, sir." James answered with a look of confusion. He glanced at Devon's expressionless face.

"Did Ray Sullivan from the Tupelo Police Department not come to your house and ask you some questions?"

"Oh, yes, sir. Yes." James shifted in the witness chair crossing his feet behind the podium. Anxiety crept over him.

"Please tell the court what you talked about." Bill Russell leaned against the witness stand.

"He came to my house and asked me the same things that Mr. Dennis just asked me, and I told him that my mother threatened my dad's life."

Devon Bradford bowed his head and smiled to himself so as not to be seen by the jury.

"James, can you identify Exhibit H?" Russell picked up the small .25 caliber gun and held it in the air.

"It's a gun my mother carried."

"To whom did it belong?"

"My father."

"How long had your mother been carrying this gun?"

"Oh, I'd say about 6 months." James leaned back in his chair.

"Did you see this gun the day your mother left?"

"No, I did not."

"I have no further questions."

Bill Russell took his seat beside Devon Bradford. He gave Devon a reassuring look. The state was going to have to do better if they were going to prove beyond a shadow of a doubt that Devon Bradford murdered his wife in cold blood.

The D. A. sat at his desk reviewing his notes. He looked at his witness sheet. Rose Smith's testimony would be important to the case since she had stated that Liz spoke with her about the argument that had taken place in the Lindenwood home. He would first hear the testimonies of Rebecca Bradford before calling Rose Smith and Liz's closest friend, Margie Bain. It would be imperative that he establish Devon as having malicious intent to kill his wife if he was going to get a conviction.

"You may call your next witness." Judge Whit motioned to Dennis. The judge smoothed his hair, a habit he could not overcome since he had begun to go bald a couple of years before. He always arrived at his destination a few minutes early to allow plenty of mirror time.

"The state calls Rebecca Bradford, Your Honor." George Dennis turned around to watch Rebecca enter the courtroom.

Rebecca walked through the swinging gate toward the witness stand. As she passed the defendant's table, she glanced at her father out of the corner of her eyes. Her frizzy, curly blond hair was pulled tightly behind her ears in a ponytail. Splotches of freckles covered her arms and face. Her eyes were a pale blue, almost white.

"Rebecca, where were you on Friday, December 20, 1974?"

"I was at home mostly." Rebecca began to pull at her ponytail. Dennis noticed her apparent nervousness.

"Who else was at home?"

"Just me and the kids."

"Who are the kids?"

"Susan and Audrey, my younger sisters."

"Were your mom and dad at home?"

"Well- my dad was working." Rebecca stuttered.

"What kind of work was your dad doing?"

"I don't know."

"Did you see or hear anything out of the ordinary that night?"

"My dad and mom were fighting, and I saw my dad hit my mom."

"Do you know why they were fighting?"

"Well, my mother had been seeing other men and my dad was upset about it." Rebecca shifted in her chair. Devon glared across the room.

"Do you know what was being said between them?" George Dennis asked with a sense of urgency.

"No, all I heard was my dad tell my mother that if he couldn't have her, nobody would." Rebecca avoided Devon's stare.

Devon's heart began to beat faster as he felt beads of sweat popping up on his neck. How could she get on the stand and screw up the entire story? She was going to hurt his case. What was she thinking? She had not listened to anything he had told her before the trial.

"Did you talk to your mother the following morning before she left?" Dennis felt he was finally getting somewhere. He noticed Devon shifting in his chair.

"No."

"Did you see her?"

"No."

"What time did she leave?"

"I guess around 11:30 or 12:00."

"Where were you when she left?"

"In my room."

"Did your mother come in your room before she left?"

"Yes, to borrow my make-up." Rebecca looked confused as she realized she had just told him she had not seen her mother that morning.

"Did you talk about anything else?"

"No." Rebecca's face was flushed.

"I have nothing further." George Dennis walked back to his table. His eyes were squinted as he thought about Rebecca's testimony. She was not going to be trustworthy. She couldn't make up her mind whether she talked to her mother on Saturday or not. And, the only thing her testimony had just done was raise more uncertainties.

"Your witness, Mr. Russell."

"Thank you." Bill Russell cleared his voice and walked from behind the defendant's table. He only had one question he wanted answered.

"Rebecca, on the Friday night before your mother's death, you stated that your mother and dad were having a fight. Were there any threats made between them of a physical nature?" Russell stared at Rebecca.

"Yes."

"Who made those threats?"

"My mother."

Eight-thirty a.m. the following morning

Monday's testimonies had not established Devon Bradford as a cold-blooded killer, but the testimonies had revealed that Liz Bradford had a reason to fear her husband. Rose Smith, who worked as a waitress with Liz Bradford at The Rex Plaza, testified later that day that Liz came to work acting very "anxious and nervous". Rose testified that Liz and Devon had been in a fight, and she had left with her clothes. Rose also testified that Liz had bruises about her neck and bald spots on her head where Devon had pulled her hair out. According to Liz, this wasn't the first time Devon had turned violent.

Margie Bain, who had been a close friend of Liz Bradford for several years, testified as a state's witness. During Margie's recollection of the events leading up to Liz's death, she informed the court that she had consoled Liz earlier that Saturday when Liz had arrived at her workplace around noon. Liz appeared to be very upset, and she showed the bruises and bald spots to Margie. She asked Margie if she could sit with her until around 5:00 p.m. when she had to report to work. Further testimony revealed that Margie had dinner with Liz later that evening, and it was during this time that Liz told her she would not need to stay the night with her. She planned on returning to Lindenwood.

George Dennis began to piece the puzzle together. Either Liz Bradford thought Devon would beg her to come home later that night, or maybe she hadn't planned on going home after all. Maybe she was going to a lover's house and didn't want her friend to know her whereabouts. The answer to that question may never be known. Dennis rubbed his head. One thing was certain. Somebody was lying or maybe everybody was lying, but why? Who was protecting who? Meanwhile, Devon Bradford was feeling confident as the day's hearing came to a close. He didn't believe the D.A. had enough evidence to prove him guilty of murder, but he was slightly concerned about Rebecca's statement. She had clearly raised doubt when she labeled her father as a wife beater, as well as indicating their marital problems. If the jury believed he killed her because of another man, he was surely doomed to the state penitentiary. He would have to find a way to get her testimony stricken from the record. It would be up to his other daughter Susan to redeem him in the eyes of the jury.

Susan Bradford, Devon's ten year-old daughter had been approved to testify in the case in spite of her age. She was known to be a "daddy's girl". Family members had often commented that she had always been Devon's favorite. Although she had already sat in the courtroom and heard her brother and sister testify, the judge would allow her to take the stand the following morning.

✝

CHAPTER 10

Susan sat quiet outside the courtroom. Her long slender legs dangled over the side of the chair as she swung her foot in borcdom. At just 10 years old, Susan already had her deceased sister Caroline's tall, thin frame which would be to her advantage as a basketball player. As she twirled her straight blondish-brown hair between her fingers, she thought of her mother the week before she was killed. She had spent a great deal of time selecting the perfect satin coin purse to give her for Christmas. Tears began to spill over her lids. The separation from her father had magnified her grief, and she detested her new living arrangements. She wanted her room back and at least part of her life with her father. The courtroom doors swung open breaking her thoughts.

"Susan Bradford, please come with me." The bailiff showed her to the witness stand. Her feet shuffled across the hardwood floors of the courtroom.

George Dennis approached the witness stand. His muscles were sore, and his eyes were red. He had not slept well the night before. He took a deep breath and looked at Susan sitting on the witness stand. Her hands rested in her lap like a puppet waiting to dance.

"Susan, you made a promise to tell the truth to all the questions we may ask you today. Do you understand the difference between a lie and telling the truth?" The D. A. spoke in a gentle manner. Because of Susan's age, he had to confirm that she understood what she was doing on the witness stand.

"Yes, sir."

District Attorney Dennis nodded. "Now, I am going to ask you some questions and these ladies and gentlemen over here are real interested in what you have to say, so I need you to speak up for them."

Susan nodded.

"Were you home on the morning your mother left?" "Yes, sir."

"Did you see or talk to her?"

"Yes, she came in my room and told me she might not see me again and kissed me."

"What time was that?"

"I don't know."

Dennis frowned. "Did you go to Tupelo later that evening?"

"Yes, sir." Susan looked at her father.

"With who?"

"With my dad. He took me Christmas shopping at Woolco, and we saw the truck mama was driving."

"Where did you see the truck?"

"I don't know exactly. It was by the post office." Susan scratched her head.

"I have no further questions." George Dennis walked back to his seat with his head down rubbing his lips. No one seemed to know what time it was when anything happened that night. His frustration was evident as he took his seat.

Bill Russell laid his pencil down and silently clapped his hands together as he approached the witness stand.

"Susan, when you and your daddy saw the truck your mother was driving, did you stop?

"Yes, sir."

"What happened then?" Russell leaned in close to the witness stand.

"I got out and peaked through the window because the doors were locked. I wanted to put mama's present in the truck."

"What did you see?" Russell held his breath. He needed her to tell the jury who had the gun marked Exhibit H.

"I saw my mother's poncho and some clothes. And her pistol was on the seat under the poncho."

Russell nodded with appreciation. That was exactly what he wanted to hear. The gun was in Liz's possession all along. He smiled to himself.

"Susan, is this the gun you saw in the truck that day?" He pointed to Exhibit H.

"Yes."

"No further questions." Russell walked back to his seat, his head high and his shoulders back. Devon

Bradford observed his attorney's self-assuredness. He wasn't impressed that his attorney was acting as if he was competing with the D.A. for best actor in a courtroom drama.

It was approximately 5:30 p. m. when Judge Whit released the dreary looking jurors for the night.

"We're going to break for this evening." Judge Whitt looked at the jurors and the two attorneys before he addressed the juror's instructions for the night.

"I realize all of you have been away from your families this week, and I'm going to allow you to call them from your motel rooms. However, you are not to call anyone else. I expect you will behave on your own good honor. This includes reading the newspaper or watching television."

Bill Russell frowned and slightly shook his head. That was asking far too much from the jurors. Human nature is human nature. Surely he didn't expect them to remember the judge's orders in the privacy of their own rooms. There could be no guarantee as to who would adhere to the rules and who wouldn't. And for those who broke the rules behind their closed motel room doors, their opinions could be swayed in the guilt or innocence of Devon Bradford.

Judge Whitt slammed the gavel down. "You're dismissed."

"All rise for the Honorable Judge Frank Whitt." The bailiff's voice was weak from fighting off the day's heat.

The jurors waited as the judge left the courtroom. Devon Bradford turned and started for the door. His face seemed to grow new wrinkles every minute. He walked slowly out of the courtroom and into the parking lot eager to get home and dreading another day closer to knowing his fate.

As soon as Devon reached Lindenwood, he went upstairs to the kitchen and prepared a sandwich. His back and legs ached from sitting for the past three days. Rebecca and James were downstairs watching television. Not knowing what would come of their dad worried them. Would they still be living at Lindenwood next week? Rebecca sat chewing her fingernails, a habit that had become worse since the loss of her mother. She hadn't slept well in the house since her mother was not there.

Memories of Liz Bradford filled the mansion. The leather belt that Devon had used to beat Liz with still lay near her bedroom door. Rebecca felt an unsettling presence each time she walked in the master suite. She had only visited her mother's grave once since the day of the funeral, but she looked out the front window each day to see the fresh dirt still piled high on the grave.

Devon walked down the stairs carrying a glass of tea. He walked over to the sofa and bent down on one knee in front of the children.

"I need to talk to you both for a minute." Devon said in his whispery tone.

"The next two days are real important for me so I need you to act real worried about your dad, okay? The jury will be looking at you. I need you to show the jury how much you need your father. Be sure and cry in the courtroom." He held Rebecca's hand. James nodded in agreement.

"Are you going to prison, Daddy?" Rebecca asked. Her voice was filled with a strange curiosity rather than concern.

"No, I don't think so. But, it's real important you do what I say, okay?" Devon looked sternly at his son and daughter.

"Okay, Daddy." Rebecca nodded. Although she agreed to do whatever her father asked, her reluctance to free her mother's killer was kept silent until her day in court.

Office of the District Attorney-9:30 p.m.

George Dennis sat behind his nineteenth century antique desk. His eyes grew heavy as he studied his latest notes. The testimonies by Dr. Jay Adams, the thoracic surgeon who operated on Devon and the testimony of Dr. William Lawson had answered several questions he had been pondering since the start of the trial. If Devon Bradford had been shot three times in the chest, how could he have been able to shoot and kill Liz Bradford?

According to Dr. Jay Adams, Devon sustained only one serious wound that penetrated a major organ. Dr. Adams informed the court that although one bullet did lodge in the lower portion of the left lung, the other two bullets passed through his body doing no major harm. Dr. Adams testified that Devon Bradford did not sustain a serious enough wound to incapacitate him from activity. He still would have been physically able to fire a gun. Dennis leaned back in his chair, rocking on the pedestal underneath.

Dr. William Lawson, who examined the body of Liz Bradford in the hospital morgue, testified that she was seriously injured from the first bullet that entered the left rear chest. This wound according to Lawson could have been fatal due to the tearing of the lower lobe of the left lung. After severing the primary artery from the heart to the lung, the bullet lodged just beneath Liz's skin. There was no way in Dr. Lawson's medical opinion that she could have physically performed any activities after this fact. If she shot Devon Bradford, she would've had to do it before she received this wound. Dennis rubbed his eyes and propped his chin in his hand, leaning forward against the desk.

"So, Liz Bradford was already dead before she received the gunshot wound to the head." He said aloud.

Dennis believed that Devon Bradford was lying. No, Devon Bradford remembered everything. Could he have shot Liz Bradford while leaning inside the car?

He tapped his fingers on his desk and began to read more of Lawson's medical reports. The second bullet entered the left back of Liz Bradford's head. According to the autopsy, it was a perfect round hole behind her left ear with the bullet tearing the brain stem and a portion of the cerebellum where it became lodged. George Dennis fidgeted in his chair trying to concentrate.

"Execution style. He put that gun right against her head and pulled the trigger." Dennis muttered to himself.

Devon must have secured the gun in order for her to be shot in this fashion. But in Devon's statement to the police, he said he had struggled over the gun and didn't remember anything else except being shot. Dennis rubbed the side of his face. Devon must have shot Liz from a standing position outside the car. That would explain why her body was found hanging over the front seat, as if she were crawling away from him. He let out a sigh and stretched his hands over his head. Tomorrow would be an even longer day with the introduction of forensic evidence. He turned off his desk lamp, grabbed his jacket, and headed out the door for home.

CHAPTER 11

At 8:30 a.m. the following morning, court resumed with the testimonies from the state crime lab and the Tupelo Police Department's detective division. Officer Roy Wilson stood in the witness box with his right hand up as he took the oath of truth.

"Officer Wilson, do you swear to tell the truth, the whole truth and nothing but the truth?"

"I do, your honor."

The D.A. stood before Wilson with a determined look on his face. "Officer Wilson, how long have you been employed by the Tupelo Police Department."

"Eight years, sir."

"Eight years. What is your title now?"

"I am a master sergeant."

"Sergeant Wilson, do you recall what time it was when you were dispatched to The Rex Plaza on December 21st, 1974?

"I would say it was close to midnight."

"What did you find when you got there?"

"I found Mr. Bradford lying face down on the parking lot. He had been shot. And I also found his wife in the front seat of a blue Chevy Impala."

Dennis pointed to the exhibit before him. "Sergeant, we have the front seat of the Chevy Impala in the courtroom. Could you please step around here and demonstrate for the jury how you found Mrs. Bradford on that night?"

Wilson stood up and stepped down from the witness box. He knelt down on the seat of the Chevy Impala, careful not to pull his knees out of joint. Wilson leaned over the back and hung his head over the armrest, his hands over his head. The jury's faces were locked in suspense. The courtroom was dead silent.

"Okay, sergeant. Thank you."

Wilson stood up, his knees cracking and popping. He walked back to the witness box and sat down.

"Sergeant, you said Mr. Bradford had been shot. How many gunshot wounds did you notice?"

"I think three."

"Did you see any gunshot wounds on Mrs. Bradford?"

"Yes."

"Do you remember where?"

"I first noticed the gunshot wound to the back of the head as she was crawling over the seat."

Russell flinched. "Your honor, I request that the court strike Sergeant Wilson's last remark from the record. He doesn't know if she was crawling over the seat. That's pure speculation."

"Okay. Officer Wilson, please rephrase your answer."

Wilson wiped his forehead. "I noticed a gunshot wound to the back of the head behind the left ear and one gunshot to the lower back." Wilson knew Devon Bradford was guilty as hell, but he also knew he probably wouldn't serve a day. He had seen it before, the guilty walking free because of a technicality.

"Anything else?"

"Yes, Mrs. Bradford appeared lifeless when we removed the body from the car. And the gun was found lying on the left side of the seat."

"That's all I have, your honor." Dennis breathed deep, fanning his face with his hand.

"Let's take a quick water break." Judge Whitt was dripping with sweat underneath the heavy cloak.

As soon as Judge Whit ordered a recess, Bill Russell dashed out of the courtroom for a water break. His shirt was moist with sweat as he paced back and forth guarding the water fountain. His mind whirled as he reviewed the morning's discoveries.

The state theorized that Devon Bradford had the gun pointed on Liz Bradford when she began to crawl over the seat. The assailant must have been on the left side of the car for the wounds to appear as they had. And Devon had told that he rode with Liz to the Pancake House before the shooting took place.

Bill Russell's head throbbed. He really didn't believe half of his client's stories most of the time, but he usually could find some errors made by police that gave him enough ammunition to win his case. But, further test results from the state crime lab had exposed false statements made by Devon Bradford. Prior to the trial, Bradford had told police that he struggled with the gun having his hands on the barrel.

Forensics confirmed there were no prints found anywhere on the barrel of the gun and according to the crime lab, either he never placed his hands on the barrel, or he wore gloves. Tests revealed that hair was found between the barrel and slide mechanism of the automatic pistol. The hair tested was proven to be human Caucasian hair from the trunk area of the body, either the chest or stomach area. The introduction of this new evidence proved crucial for the state's argument that Devon Bradford had shot himself.

Attorney Bill Russell sighed heavily. With diligence, he had attempted to dispute each point made by the state crime lab. His forehead was beaded with sweat. He wiped his face with his monogrammed handkerchief he kept shoved in his pocket. His wife had given him a set of the handkerchiefs years ago when he started his practice. He carried one with him daily saying 'the damn humidity made it a necessity'.

Devon Bradford glided into the lobby. He noticed Russell pacing back and forth.

"Mr. Russell, can I offer you a cigarette?" Devon looked at Russell expecting him to reveal what was bothering him. He reached in his pocket, pulling two of the sticks from a new pack of Winston's.

"No thanks. It's just so damn hot in here. Those damn fans aren't getting the job done in that courtroom." Russell wiped more sweat from his brow.

"Yes, sir. It's just about unbearable. So, how do you think we stand after this morning?" Devon changed the subject and propped one hand against the wall.

"Well, I don't think you should worry. I believe my questioning of that detective Bobby Johnson pretty much ruined the state crime lab's testimony. Remember, Johnson said he secured hair samples from the body that were given to him by the funeral home director in charge of Liz's burial, but he said he kept some of the scene's evidence in his desk drawer. He couldn't prove that the evidence hadn't been tampered with."

"Yeah, but why didn't the judge dismiss the bullet hulls and hair samples after hearing that? That Johnson fellow had already stated that he never even sent the samples to Jackson. He kept them in a sealed envelope in his desk drawer."

Russell threw his hands up in disgust. "I don't know. I swear I don't. Seems like he just turned his damn head and looked the other way."

Devon stared at Russell with his head tilted sideways as if he had spoken to him in a foreign language.

"You know if they convict me, I'm appealing this. I will appeal this case until I'm free." Devon's tone emphasized his unwillingness to go to prison. He flicked cigarette ashes in his hand and took another long drag.

Russell looked at him and realized it may be awhile before he rested. He noticed the dark circles under Devon's eyes from lack of sleep.

"We will do whatever it takes, Mr. Bradford." Russell gave Devon a reassuring pat on the shoulder and walked off, headed for the restroom.

Russell continued to think about the prosecution's attempt to prove that Liz had been shot at close range. Police reports stated that she had powder burns on her head. But, the autopsy records contradicted police reports saying there weren't any powder burns found. According to the state crime lab, powder burns are left on the skin only if the gun is fired no more than eighteen inches away. Without hard proof from the autopsy, the state simply could not prove Devon Bradford had shot his wife at close range as they had proposed all along.

Russell stood over the basin filling with cold water. He cupped some water in his hand, splashing it on his face to cool himself. He grabbed a paper towel and patted his forehead as he walked out the door headed back to the courtroom. Just as he stepped inside the courtroom doors, James Bradford ran over to him pulling at his arm.

"Mr. Russell, I've got to talk to you," James was breathless, his pale blue eyes wide.

"What's the problem?" Russell stopped what he was doing and paid attention.

"That doctor said my mother didn't have any powder burns on her but she did! I saw them!"

Russell's eyes were steady as he studied James's face. "What do you mean you saw them?"

"I mean- I saw my mother. I saw the powder burns."

"Wait right here." Russell walked out of the courtroom in a rush. He had to find Judge Whit. He motioned for the D.A. to follow him.

"What's going on?" Dennis called out to Russell as he grabbed the door handle.

Russell shook his head and turned his hands up as if he didn't know. He whispered loudly to the D.A. "James Bradford says he saw his mother on ice in the morgue."

"Do what?" Dennis raced to Russell's side as they both entered the judge's chambers.

Judge Whitt was fanning his face and drinking a glass of iced tea. "What's going on?" Whitt leaned forward in his chair.

Russell's throat was dry causing him to cough. "Your honor, James Bradford has approached me in the lobby with some news about his mother's condition."

"Go on." Whitt listened with interest, his head tilted to the side.

"He says he saw his mother on ice. In the morgue. He says he saw the bullet holes."

The judge held up his hand. "Bring him in here. I want him to tell me what he saw."

Russell left Dennis and Judge Whitt behind chambers as he rushed out to find James Bradford. He opened the doors to the lobby and found James leaning against the wall waiting for the attorney.

"James, come with me, please. The judge wants to hear what you have to say in his chambers."

Russell showed James to the small room and closed the heavy wooden doors behind him.

"Go ahead, Bill." Judge Whit instructed Russell to begin his questioning.

"James, we're going to ask you a few questions for the record, and I want you to tell the judge exactly what you just told me, okay?"

James nodded in agreement. His palms began to sweat and his mouth became dry.

"You understand that you are still under oath?"

"Yes, sir."

"James, have you ever talked to me outside this courtroom?"

"No, sir." James looked puzzled.

"Did you not just come up to me a few minutes ago outside?" Russell asked annoyed, his eyebrows in a furrow.

"Oh, yes, sir. Yes."

"Tell the judge what you told me, please."

"I told Mr. Russell that there were powder burns on my mother's head because I saw them."

"Where did you see your mother?"

"On ice."

"On ice?" Russell asked with surprise.

"Yes, sir at the hospital morgue."

"How did you get into the morgue?" Russell doubted him.

"When I went to the hospital the next morning after the shooting, I tried to see my father, but they wouldn't let me, so I went downstairs to the morgue to see if I could see my mother. And I kept bugging them until they let me in."

"What happened then?" Russell looked over at the D.A. who was leaning against a chair.

"I went in and stood over my mother who was on ice, and I picked up her head and turned it over. I moved the hair back from behind her ear, and I saw the bullet hole with powder burns on her skin."

Bill Russell and George Dennis stared at Judge Whit in anticipation. Would he allow James's testimony before the jury?

"I'll allow this as part of the record behind chambers, but we won't introduce it to the jury at this time." Judge Whit glanced over at Russell who was frowning with disapproval.

Russell had to accept the judge's decision. He walked out of the chambers with his jaw clenched tight. Russell realized this testimony could be detrimental in proving that Devon Bradford had to have struggled with Liz Bradford over the gun when it fired at close range. Disgusted, he slammed his briefcase shut and walked out of the courtroom.

✝

CHAPTER 12

Devon Bradford woke with knots in his stomach. It was 5:00 a.m., just hours away from the final day of his trial. He knew he had to testify. He had practiced his speech over and over in his mind careful not to make a mistake. Bill Russell had not said much to him after court the day before. He got out of bed and walked upstairs to make his morning coffee. He would have about five cups and smoke half a pack of cigarettes before he ever made it to the courthouse.

"Mr. Dennis, are you ready to call your next witness?" Judge Whit wiped his forehead that already glistened with sweat. The June days in the South continued to heat the poorly ventilated courtroom.

"Yes, your honor. The state calls Devon Bradford." George Dennis turned to watch Devon as he walked to the witness stand. He walked with a sense of humility, slow and easy. His face was without expression. He knew he had to win the jury's favor, and he had tried to prepare himself for the witness stand. He sat down in the hard, wooden chair and waited for the D.A.

"Mr. Bradford, place your right hand on the Bible." Devon stood and placed his hand on the Bible, his head held high.

"Do you swear to tell the truth, the whole truth, so help you God?"

Devon nodded. "I do." He glanced at the jury box as he eased into his chair.

"I'm going to ask you some questions about the night the shooting occurred." Dennis waited for Devon to indicate he understood. Devon nodded.

"On the Friday night before the shooting, you stated that you and your wife were having an argument, is that right?" "Yes, that's right."

"Were there any threats made on that night?"

"No. Not that I recall."

"Were there any physical blows exchanged?"

Devon looked at his hands with his head turned to one side. "Well, we had our share of fights like any other married couple and if she pulled my hair, I pulled hers."

"So, are you saying you never struck your wife that night?"

"No, I did not."

"You did not hit her or strike her with a belt?"

"No, absolutely not." Devon frowned shaking his head.

"Where did your wife sleep that night, Mr. Bradford?" "In the den. On the couch."

"Did you see her the next morning?"

"Well- Devon fidgeted in his seat. I got up around 6:00 and saw her sleeping or playing like she was."

"What happened then?"

"I went to town and bought some parts to fix the car, and then I started working on it when I got home."

"What time did your wife leave the house?"

"I don't know. Maybe around lunch."

"Did you see her?"

"Not until she came out of the house and began loading the truck with clothes."

"Did you talk to her?"

"I asked her where she was going, and she told me she was leaving and for me to bring the car to her later at work since all my work tools were on the truck."

"Mr. Bradford, later that day you stated that you went Christmas shopping with your daughter. Tell me about that, please."

"My daughter, Susan asked if I would take her shopping to pick up some gifts she needed to take to school, and so we left and went to Tupelo that afternoon."

"Where did you go?"

"She wanted to go to Woolco. So, I took her there."

"How far is Woolco from the post office downtown?"

"I don't know. Not far, though." Devon wondered where the D.A. was leading him.   "Did you not find your wife's truck parked downtown that afternoon?"

"No."

"Tell me what you did next."

"After I got home, I laid down for a nap. Then I got up and I guess it was around 10:00 p.m. when I left to come to Tupelo."

"What happened when you got to The Rex Plaza?"

"I saw that the restaurant was already closed so I went around to the lobby entrance and peeped in the window where I saw my wife standing in the hall. She saw me and came outside where I was. She then asked me where I was parked and told me to pull the car around to the front of the building so she could put her clothes in the car. I moved the car, and we started talking some."

Devon looked blankly at the D.A.

"Is there anything more?"

"She asked me to go to the Pancake House for some coffee, and I said okay. She got in the car and offered me a cigarette. She drove us to the Pancake House and it was real crowded, so I told her I had changed my mind, and I wanted to go home because I didn't feel well, so she drove us back to The Rex Plaza."

"Was there any arguing going on?"

"We were fussing a little."

"What happened when you got back to the motel?"

"Well, I went to get out of the car and when I turned I felt a real hard push. I fell against the door and started trying to get out."

"What do you mean? Were you pushed?"

"No, my wife shot me."

"What exactly had happened prior to you being shot?"

"We were fighting and all of a sudden she said 'here is a gift you won't ever forget' and then she shot me." A cold sweat began to sweep over Devon. He felt trapped.

George Dennis stood quiet for a moment contemplating his next move. Devon Bradford hadn't really given any new information that he didn't already know except he lied about seeing Liz Bradford's truck earlier that day. Why he lied was unknown, but according to his ten-year old daughter he had driven by the vehicle and stopped so she could look in the window. Dennis looked hard at Devon.

"Mr. Bradford, you stated to the police that you struggled with your wife after you saw the gun. Please tell the court about your struggle."

"Uh, well, when my wife brought the gun around, she pointed it at my head, and I started to knock her hand away and grabbed the gun trying to keep her from shooting me. But I got shot anyway. I don't-"I don't remember anything after that."

"No further questions." Dennis walked back to his desk. He scanned the notes that Oliver had prepared.

"Your witness, Mr. Russell." Judge Whitt watched Russell as he approached the witness stand.

Russell's lips were pursed as he walked to the witness stand. "Mr. Bradford, did you love your wife?"

"Yes, and I don't think-

"Please tell me again what happened when you got back to The Rex Plaza."

"Well, we had talked a little bit going down to the Pancake House and on the way back, and she said something or other about-- 'that could I have just'-

"Could it please the Court- Could I have a break, about a two minute break?" Devon was distraught. His stomach began to churn. He felt a chill as beads of sweat popped out on his face. He had to think fast.

"Are you feeling alright, Mr. Bradford?" Judge Whitt looked down at the witness stand.

Devon shook his head. He had to get outside and get his thoughts together. If he messed this up, he could go to prison.

"Just a couple of minutes will help. I just need some fresh air."

"Let's take a brief five minute recess." Judge Whitt left the bench headed for the water cooler in his office.

Devon walked outside with the bailiff. His hands trembled as he lit a cigarette. With each puff, his head throbbed. He had not been prepared for this line of questioning. Devon took one last drag and flicked the cigarette butt on the courthouse step. He rubbed his forehead hard as he wiped off the sweat of pure fear. He walked back into the courtroom. All eyes were on him as he took the witness stand, clearing his voice as he sat down.

"Mr. Bradford, let's resume where we left off. You were telling us about the struggle with your wife at The Rex Plaza."

"My wife said, 'here's you a present that you won't never forget and she had her-and when I made my turn-she pulled the trigger and I fell back against the door of the car."

"Mr. Bradford, to whom did that gun belong?"

"It was mine, but she-"

"And where did you get it?"

"I got it several years ago when I lived in Kansas. A man gave it to me."

"No further questions, your honor."

"We're going to break for a couple of hours. Court is adjourned until 2 p.m." Judge Whitt slammed the gavel down and walked toward his chambers eager to escape the heat of the courtroom.

George Dennis felt refreshed after lunch having had two huge glasses of sweet ice tea from the local deli. He sat in the empty courtroom behind his table and reviewed his closing arguments. He believed that Devon Bradford had not only committed murder, but had planned to do it when he went to his wife's workplace on that Saturday night. But in order to get a conviction, he must prove that Devon Bradford had exercised malicious aforethought with intent to kill his wife. The evidence was too circumstantial. Russell would probably argue in light of this fact, and therefore insist that the charge of murder be withdrawn from the verdict. The state's strongest evidence of murder lay in the position of Liz Bradford's body and the state crime lab's testimonies, but Dennis knew he had not proven that Devon Bradford planned the death of his wife. He let out a sigh and looked at his watch. It was only thirty more minutes before court would resume.

Dennis heard the familiar footsteps of his friend and co-hort, Richard Oliver. His steps were heavy on the wooden floors as if he were wearing boots. Oliver slowed as he approached the door to Dennis's office. He stood with his hand resting in the doorframe. Oliver took a deep breath.

"Well, this one is about over. I think it seems pretty cut and dry if you ask me, but I'm not sure how the jury is gonna vote." Oliver looked at Dennis leaning back in his chair.

"Oh yeah, it's cut and dry all right. You believe this guy is guilty?" Dennis asked the question with more of an affirmation as he studied Oliver brushing the dust from his polished black shoes.

"As hell. But, there were no witnesses and the police department's screwy way of handling the evidence shot a hole in this case. I think we gave it our best shot with what we had, but I guarantee you, this Bradford fellow ain't going to prison for murder."

"Nope. If we're lucky, manslaughter." Dennis wiped his face.

Oliver suddenly stood straight. "Hey, did you realize that he was lying on the stand?"

"Which time?" Dennis looked up at his friend as if he had asked a stupid question.

"When he was talking about coming to Tupelo the day of the murder. You remember his daughter said that she saw the pistol on the front seat of the truck when they stopped to put a present in the seat, but he said he never went downtown. I don't think the kid was lying."

Dennis shook his head. "No, no. He was. I would even guess that he got the gun and had it all along. How else did it end up in the car?" Oliver rubbed his fingers through his hair. He took his glasses off and chewed on the frame then pointed them toward Dennis.

"You know, everything that guy said on the witness stand seemed to be the opposite of what I picture happened. His testimony also contradicted the children's testimony. I think *he* had that gun and put it to *her* head."

"Me too." Dennis rolled back in his chair and began to stand. He took a deep breath then exhaled slowly.

Oliver dropped his hands and started to walk back down the hall. He turned and called over his shoulder. "But, it doesn't matter what we think, George."

Dennis silently agreed as he grabbed his suit coat from the back of the chair and flicked off the light.

***

Back in the courtroom two hours later...

The district attorney walked around the table and surveyed the jurors as he approached the jury box. He attempted to read each of their thoughts. His closing argument had to convince them beyond a shadow of a doubt that Devon Bradford was a killer. Dennis feared the evidence was just not solid enough. There were no witnesses except Liz Bradford, and she was buried six feet under. It would be up to him to tell the jury what she wanted them to know.

Judge Whit motioned for the D.A. to proceed. Dennis stood with one hand resting on the ledge of the jury box and the other in his pocket.

"Ladies and Gentlemen of the jury, Liz Bradford cannot be here to tell you what happened to her on the night of December 22, 1974, but as her defender, I can." He paused and looked at the jury with intent and purpose.

"Just three days before Christmas when she would have spent the morning opening Santa with her children, Liz Bradford left her home and went to work after being beaten the night before by her husband, Devon Bradford. Her head was bruised. Her scalp had bald spots where Mr. Bradford had pulled her hair out by the roots. She worked that night, tired and an emotional wreck waiting on customers in the restaurant of The Rex Plaza. Her suitcase was packed and sitting in her boss's office at the lounge. Later that evening around 10:00 to 10:30 p.m., Devon Bradford arrived at the motel. He waited on Mrs. Bradford to get off work. He walked her to her car where he asked her to go with him to the Pancake House for a cup of coffee."

"You will remember that Mr. Bradford testified that it was *Mrs. Bradford* who insisted on going for coffee, but I believe it was Mr. Bradford *himself* who coaxed her into leaving the Inn, and I believe it was not *him* but *her* that insisted the place was too crowded to stay. Why would Liz Bradford want to talk to her husband about coming home if she had already packed her bags? It was Mr. Bradford who had driven to Tupelo to confront her, not the other way around. *She* was leaving *him*."

Dennis walked in a half circle rubbing his lips.

"When Mr. and Mrs. Bradford were in that car at The Rex Plaza, there was a struggle. Mr. Bradford testified that Mrs. Bradford pulled a gun on him and said, 'Here's a present you'll never forget.'" Now as I recollect, we all heard the testimony of Susan Bradford who told that she saw the pistol lying in the seat of the truck earlier in the day, but according to testimony Devon and Liz Bradford were never in the truck together. I believe Devon Bradford moved that pistol before he ever saw his wife that evening. Mrs. Bradford asked her husband to pull the car around so she could move her clothes from the truck to the car. It doesn't make sense that Liz Bradford would have carried the pistol into her workplace where she felt safe and secure from her husband. We know Mr. Bradford was on the motel grounds before Mrs. Bradford got off work because he went in the lounge area and asked the bartender her whereabouts."

Dennis looked at the jurors. Each member listened intently as he continued to paint a picture straight from the mouth of Liz Bradford's grave.

"The struggle that ended in Liz Bradford's death was not an accident. Mr. Bradford had a history of striking his wife. That night he not only struck her, he held a gun to her head and told her 'if I can't have you, no one will'. It was then that Liz Bradford struggled with him and managed to discharge the pistol three times into her husband's chest area, but it wasn't enough to stop him. She desperately began to climb over the front seat of the Chevy Impala. Her arms and head were bent over the armrest in a fleeing position when she received the first bullet wound to the back and then another behind her left ear. Devon Bradford went to The Rex Plaza to bring his cheating wife home by force and intimidation. In the end, she came back to Lindenwood in a box leaving behind five children to live the rest of their lives without a mother."

Dennis stopped and looked around the courtroom. "The only person fighting for their life on December 21st, 1974 was Liz Bradford. Now, I ask each of you to enter a guilty plea for Devon Bradford in the name of justice. Allow Liz Bradford to rest in peace." Dennis stood with his hands clasped together covering his mouth as he beckoned each member with his eyes. He then turned his back and hoped he had made the jury see Liz's real fate. It seemed as if the day had been an illusion as the clock finally reached 5:30 p.m. Dennis felt he had presented the evidence as best as he could and knew it would be up to the jury to decide Devon Bradford's fate. One way or another, he was ready to get out of the blistering heat of the courtroom.

Russell's closing argument was quick and precise, but he was still not so eager to be done. He had his reputation on the line. He reasoned that there was no way he could lose the case with the testimony that had been given and the poor case that the state had presented. Too many things had been fouled up from the beginning of the crime scene. He had asked the jury to withdraw the charge of murder, but Devon could still be charged with manslaughter. At least it carried a lighter sentence if all else failed. But, Russell's work wasn't done yet. Judge Whit still held a new surprise for him when he made a decision that not only upset Devon Bradford but could have decided his fate.

Whit cleared his voice and pushed his glasses up the bridge of his nose. "I'm going to dismiss the jury for the evening. We'll resume court at 8:30 a.m. tomorrow morning for the final verdict." He looked at the box of jurors who unanimously breathed a sigh of relief.

"I expect that all of you could use some rest and relaxation tonight, and that is what I want you to do. I am leaving you again on your good honor with regards to the media attention in this case. You may have access to the telephone and television, but you know what is expected of you. Have a good night." He hammered the gavel once.

Devon Bradford jerked at Russell's arm. "He can't do that. If he lets them go home for the night and think about it, it could hurt my case. Why can't we finish this tonight?"

Russell jumped up from his seat. "Your honor, my client respectfully asks that we finish his case this evening."

Whit looked at Russell without sympathy. "I understand Mr. Bradford's eagerness to put this behind him, but I also understand the jurors need for a night of contemplation and relaxation. Your request is denied. I'll see you tomorrow morning."

8:30 a.m. the following morning~

Will the defendant please rise?" The bailiff spoke loud and clear. Judge Whit held his hands clasped together as he looked at the faces of the jury and Devon Bradford.

"Madam Juror, has the jury reached a verdict?"

"Yes, sir, we have." The juror handed the bailiff a folded piece of paper. He passed the paper to Judge Whit.

Devon Bradford took a deep breath as he stood up from his chair. He looked around the courtroom studying the faces of the jurors. He thought he might be able to tell which way they were leaning by the expression on their faces, but everyone stood quiet and solemn as the judge opened the small note he held in his hand. Judge Whit scanned the courtroom looking at the benches filled with family members and friends of the deceased as well as Devon Bradford. He spoke loud, commanding and authoritative.

"Before the verdict is read, I want to make it clear to everyone in the courtroom that I expect total silence. There will be no comments or emotional displays tolerated."

"You may go ahead, Madam Juror."

Every person in the room held their breath. Devon's children and family sat squeezing one another's hands as the family of Liz Bradford sat with their hands in a prayer position hoping to appease their loved one's death. All eyes were on the juror as she lifted the paper in front of her face and made the announcement everyone was waiting for.

"We, the jury, find the defendant guilty of manslaughter."

✟

CHAPTER 13

Nine months had passed. The warm April days had begun to coax Devon Bradford out of hiding. He had not socialized much since his trial. After the State Supreme Court overturned his verdict, the D.A. was ordered to re-try the case. Devon had no intention of serving one day for Liz Bradford's death and didn't care what he had to do to stay out of prison. Russell knew they had a chance because of the foul up with the evidence. The State Supreme court had not hesitated to overturn the verdict, and that could only mean he would be a free man.

Devon stood staring at his reflection in the mirror of the small master bath. The bright light above the sink illuminated the area far more than he was accustomed to since he had installed dimmer switches throughout the house when it was built. Devon rubbed his hand over his cheek feeling the black hair stubble that covered his face. He studied his face wondering if the stubble gave him a sexier look. He would be going to The Rex Plaza tonight, and he had to look his best. It didn't matter to him that his wife had worked there or even that it was where she lay dead by his hands only a few months ago. It was the classiest place around and the best place to meet single, good-looking women, especially vulnerable women.

Dressed in a white button down shirt and black dress pants, Devon looked incredibly handsome. His chest was hidden beneath a white wife beater tank shirt that he always wore to cover the generous amount of chest hair he had inherited. He admired his firm jaw and rugged good looks. His nose was a little large for his face, but he felt he had so much else going for him that it didn't matter. The nose was just a matter of distinction. He turned the dimmer knob down on the light switch and grabbed the keys from the nightstand as he walked out the door.

Fifteen miles away in a small cramped bathroom, the operating room nurse that had helped save Devon Bradford's life took a break from rolling her lustrous auburn hair long enough to smoke a cigarette. She still had forty-five minutes left to finish getting ready, and even though she would look the image of a red-haired princess, Natalie Houston figured she was wasting her time. She spent most of her time in front of the mirror discovering new faults. She believed her large breasts made her look too fat, her hips were too full, and her eyes were too big. In reality, it was her eyes that captivated men time and time again, but if she wasn't ridiculing her looks, she was spending time hating herself for past mistakes. She stood in the closet door thumbing through several blouses before making a choice. The Rex Plaza was the hottest spot in town, and she wanted to look irresistible. She finished dressing and paid special attention as she applied make-up to her deep-set green eyes. She applied the same Cover Girl lipstick that she always wore in a brown, frosty color. She grabbed a tissue and blotted her slightly full lips.

"Anna, get your bag. We're ready to go."

"Are you taking me to Grandma's?" Anna Houston stood in the doorway holding a pink suitcase barely big enough to hold a pair of shoes much less a change of clothes. "Yes, honey. Go get in the car."

Anna slowly climbed into the blue Oldsmobile. Although Natalie frequently went out on the town, the seven year-old dreaded her leaving. She clung to Natalie, and like an infant, she longed to see and smell her mother's hair when she embraced her at the end of a workday. The twenty-minute ride to Sarah Cooper's was quiet. Sarah had been a widow since the late 1960's and didn't mind telling anyone that she never wanted another man as long as she lived. She seemed quite content living on 'her hill' with a few acres to garden and a catfish pond she frequented in the afternoons. If she wasn't working in the garden, she was studying her Bible and had read it cover to cover several times. As Natalie turned into the gravel drive, Anna beamed at her grandmother standing on the front porch of the cottage style house. She bolted out of the car and ran up the steps. Natalie rolled down the window.

"Mother, I'm not going to get out. I'm running a little late."

"Okay, be careful. We'll see you tomorrow."

Sarah waved as the car disappeared on the dusty gravel road. She shook her head wishing that her daughter would get in church and stop the nonsense that was only causing her trouble. She couldn't understand why Natalie chased men. The truth was that Natalie was searching for something, but it was the search that had led her to a hellish life.

As Natalie changed the radio tune, she turned her thoughts back to the night out on the town that was awaiting her. She had heard there might be a bachelor or two at The Rex Plaza, and she was eager to meet her friend Margaret. She wasn't looking for a relationship since she had only been divorced from her second husband for a few months, but flirting was always fun to her and she enjoyed the nightlife of the Lion's Den.

Thirty minutes passed before Natalie pulled into the motel parking lot. The crowd had already gathered, and the lot was almost full. Several cars already lined the front of the lounge entrance. Dusk had already settled in the city, and the brass lanterns hanging outside the lounge doors were buzzing as they flickered on.

Natalie carefully parked her car in the back parking lot. She turned off the ignition and picked up the beaded purse from the seat beside her. As she got out of the car and began her way up the dimly lit sidewalk, her friend Margaret York, waved from the backdoor to the bar.

"Hey, Nat, over here." Margaret held the door. She looked the part of an aristocrat with her red, beaded cocktail dress and shiny high heel shoes. She took a drag on her cigarette with a tortoise shell filter on the end.

"We'll have to get you one of these." She clinked the ice cubes in the glass and held it high.

"Sounds great. I'm ready, girl. Where's the booze?" Natalie gave Margaret a wicked, mischievous grin. The sound of Elvis's *Burning Love* could be heard from inside the lounge. The air was warm and breezy, just right for attracting patrons to The Rex Plaza for dancing and socializing. Natalie smiled as she reached for the door handle. As she opened the door to the bar area, she was flooded with the sweet smell of a cigar. The lights were dim in the lounge creating a romantic, sultry atmosphere. The lounge was decorated in red plush carpet and black and white checkered ceramic tile. The bar area sparkled with crystal wine and champagne stems hanging overhead. Martini stems hung overhead to the right of the bar. Crystal ashtrays lined the bar, each one sparkling clean within seconds of being soiled. On each end of the bar were silver baskets lined with fresh linens to hold nuts and pretzels.

Natalie followed Margaret to the bar. She climbed on a barstool and searched her purse for a cigarette. Margaret took a seat next to Natalie. Margaret leaned over to Natalie's ear. "Did you see the dark-haired guy at the end of the bar? He's staring a hole through you."

Margaret's voice was barely loud enough to be heard over the music.

"Yeah, of course I noticed. I'm a sucker for dark men, you know." She looked at Margaret as if she had asked a question she already knew the answer to.

Margaret nodded and took a drag on her cigarette. She crossed her legs, gently swinging her foot at the ankle and glanced around the room. Several men sat together in a corner of the bar talking loud and smoking cigars. As Natalie joined her friend in surveying the room, Devon Bradford leaned back in his chair at the end of the bar and watched Natalie Houston's every move.

His eyes were quick to avoid her gaze while he was summing her up. He looked as if he were a lion studying his prey until just the right moment. His eyes were half closed, his head down. He pretended to be looking at the half empty glass of whiskey, but the corner of his eyes was fixed on the auburn brunette across the room. Her presence was familiar to him. There was something about her that puzzled him. She reminded him of someone he knew, but who?

He studied her voluptuous hips and generous bust line. His loins stirred at the thought of being with a woman again. It had been months since he had known sexual ecstasy. Visions of his intimacy with Liz Bradford flashed through his mind. It was the only thing about his deceased wife that he could admit that he missed. Maybe it was the brunette's physical attributes that reminded him of Liz Bradford. Or perhaps it was her outward persona that shouted her vulnerability that really attracted him. Reading women was easy for

Devon Bradford. He had spent years perfecting his art, and it was the one tool that was essential in capturing his prey. Like a sociopath, he had to learn his victim's one weakness. Like many lonely women, Natalie's weakness was always obvious. She needed a man's adoration to feel complete. Her weakness was her lack of self-love.

Ben Johnson stood behind the bar cleaning an ashtray for the hundredth time. His sleeves were rolled up twice on his crisp, white button down shirt. His black bow tie was untied and hanging down the front of his shirt. He watched the end of the bar for a moment summing up the dark-haired man he had seen before in the restaurant. Devon Bradford was unaware the bartender had eyes on him.

Ben mumbled to himself, "I can't believe the nerve of that guy." He remembered the waitress that had worked for his stepfather at the motel, and he remembered the night she had been murdered on his lot. He shook his head in disbelief at the thought of Devon Bradford coming back to the place where Liz Bradford had worked and had been murdered. Unease swept over Natalie as she felt the eyes of Devon Bradford on her. Her keen sense of her surroundings was in overdrive as it almost always was, even though she was too quick to brush aside intuitive warnings. She slipped off the barstool and made her way to the ladies room. If she passed by the handsome man, maybe he would stop her. She cleared her voice and casually walked past him.

Devon sat against the barstool with one leg outstretched and the other foot resting on the bottom of the stool. One arm was stretched over the back of the stool while he rested his elbow on the corner of the bar. His eyes followed Natalie, enveloping her body as she walked. Devon's deep, piercing eyes penetrated her body and hypnotized her as she stared back before giving him an inviting smile.

Natalie blinked, studying the face of Devon Bradford whose slight grin had turned into a hungry look of desire. She stood still looking at the stranger who was partially hidden in the dim light. Her heart began to flutter as he stepped forward to greet her.

Devon extended his hand. "Hey, Scarlet, what are you drinking tonight?" His presence was warm bathing over her body.

He gazed at Natalie, taking in her facial features as he admired her deep-set green eyes and round firm breasts. He noticed Natalie's shyness and awkward degree of vulnerability without her friend by her side. Her composure had taken a fast turn as she spoke in a gentle and ultra-feminine voice.

"Red wine. If you'll excuse me, I'll be right back." Natalie rushed for the ladies room. She took a deep breath. His rugged good looks overwhelmed her, and he had called her Scarlet. She couldn't imagine being compared to Vivien Leigh.

Devon ordered a couple of drinks and guarded a barstool beside his. When Natalie returned, she eased beside him and climbed on the stool.

"I don't think I've introduced myself. I'm Devon Bradford." He extended his hand for a soft handshake. He undressed her with his eyes.

Natalie lavished the attention she was getting from a man like Devon Bradford, a man well-groomed and sophisticated. He must be successful and have many female admirers. She placed her hand in his.

"I'm Natalie Houston." Her green eyes glistened under the soft glow of burning candles.

"Are you here with someone?" Devon couldn't take his eyes off her. He was eager to find out if she was available, but he didn't really care if she wasn't.

"No, No. I came with a girlfriend." Natalie smiled at him and sipped her wine.

Devon continued to keep Natalie's glass full ordering the wine as soon as she managed to drink a half glass. As the hour ticked away, the alcohol seemed to bring out a more confident, sexual woman in her. But, the alcohol's intoxicating effect was no match for the effect that Devon Bradford would have on her. He had been without a woman for several months and was eager to satisfy his manly need.

Margaret York glanced at Natalie several times during the hour. She wondered who the new admirer was that had captivated her friend. She had known Natalie for years, and she knew how easy her friend could get involved with the wrong man. Natalie was tragic in many ways, seeking a fairy tale romance with anyone willing to entertain her with their illusion. Margaret put her glass down on the bar and turned to find her friend. She approached the two with a wide grin, her front teeth noticeable by a slight gap between them.

"Natalie, who is your new friend?" Margaret leaned over to shake Devon's hand. Her eyes roamed his face.

Natalie noticed Margaret eyeing Devon and felt a sudden twinge of jealously. "This is Devon Bradford."

Margaret continued to stare at Devon, envious of Natalie's sudden catch. "I'm Margaret York." Her large bangle bracelets clanked together as she extended her hand and smoothed her blond hair with the other.

Devon nodded a hello. "Pleased to meet you."

"Do you live in Tupelo, Devon?" Margaret turned her head sideways and smiled playing the part of a sweet, southern belle.

"No, I'm not from here."

"Oh, really, where are you from?"

Devon coughed and looked down at the floor. He wanted her to get lost. He wasn't interested in talking to her any longer, but he knew he had to be polite. He didn't like telling too many people who he was because of his recent trial. If Margaret had heard about it in the news, she might tell Natalie and ruin his chance with her.

"I own the Lindenwood home a few miles from here." He turned his attention back to Natalie. "Join me for a dance?" Devon stood taking Natalie's hand.

"You are the Devon Bradford of Lindenwood?" She asked interrupting again. Her face turned pale as if she had seen a ghost.

Devon frowned and cursed to himself. "Yep, that's me." He pulled Natalie close, ignoring Margaret as he led Natalie into a crowd of shaking hips on the dance floor.

Margaret froze where she stood. The much talked about Devon Bradford was at The Rex Plaza, the same Devon Bradford that had supposedly killed his wife at the motel just last year. She had heard he had a habit of controlling women and didn't take kindly to rejection. She knew Natalie Houston would be his next target, and she figured he had probably picked up on Natalie's weaknesses. She would be easy for him. Margaret York felt a chill as she watched him charm her friend, sucking her into a hellish nightmare.

✝

CHAPTER 14

Natalie walked the long halls of the south wing at North Mississippi Medical Center. It was break time. That meant eating a plate lunch in the hospital cafeteria and smoking a cigarette with her friend, Margaret York. She swung the door open to the lounge and flopped down on the sofa next to Margaret.

Margaret looked at her love struck friend. "Nat, I need to tell you something."

Natalie sighed. She had a feeling Margaret was going to start lecturing her about Devon. She was always jealous of her new boyfriends if she didn't have one.

"Okay, but let's eat first. You ready?"

"Yeah, sure." Margaret noticed Natalie wasn't interested in what she had to say. But, she wasn't surprised. She was on her second divorce and falling head over heels in love with a killer. Margaret had to warn her even if she didn't listen this time. She had to know that she had tried to steer her friend out of danger.

The two women followed behind a crowd of other hungry hospital workers dressed in lab coats and white uniforms as they made their way to the cafeteria. They filled their plates and took a table near the corner of the room. Natalie pulled her cigarettes out of her white lab jacket. She flicked the lighter on and puffed on a Marlboro as if she were in ecstasy. Margaret played with her pasta, twirling the fork around the edge of the bowl.

"Listen, I think you need to know something." Margaret paused and looked at Natalie with her chin resting in her hand.

"I'll listen to you, I promise." Natalie said in a teasing tone.

Margaret put her fork down and reached for a cigarette, eager to join in the smoking scene.

"I have heard some stories about Devon Bradford. Now, I'm not saying everything is true that I'm going to tell you, but it doesn't hurt to have your eyes wide open."

"I know what you're going to say. That he killed his wife." Natalie rolled the cigarette around the edge of the ashtray, a habit since she started smoking in nurse's school.

"And you don't believe it?" Margaret looked at Natalie dumbfounded.

"No, Margaret. I have been seeing Devon for over four weeks now, and he is the kindest man I've ever met. He loves my children, and he wants me to be a mother to his. What I can't believe is why Liz Bradford cheated on him." Natalie's eyes were full of admiration for Devon.

"What has he told you about Liz?"

"He told me how she took that job at The Rex Plaza so she could be away from him and the kids. He said she never wanted to be a wife and mother. Then he found out she was seeing a man she had met at work."

Margaret leaned forward and whispered.

"Nat, I don't know the Bradfords, but I do know that Liz Bradford was beaten by this man before she was shot. Now, I'm telling you- just be careful."

Natalie looked around the room to see if anyone noticed them whispering. "I think you're just paranoid. Or, maybe you're just jealous." Her tone was inquisitive.

Margaret laughed. "Why the hell do you always do that? I'm not going without, sweetheart. I'm just trying to be your friend. Don't read into it."

Natalie shrugged. "I'm going to give him the benefit of the doubt. I really like him." She pointed her finger at Margaret. "But, if you're right, I want you to save your damn lectures."

Margaret nodded. "Don't worry. I'll be so relieved that you listened to common sense this time, I'll forget all about it." She brushed her hand in the air and looked at Natalie sideways. "So, have you met his children?"

"Not yet, but tomorrow night he's taking me to Lindenwood. I can't wait. I've heard it's beautiful."

"Rich is what it is. And haunted." Margaret drank the watered down tea in her glass. She remembered the graveyard facing Lindenwood. "Hey, did you know his ex-wife and daughter are buried across the highway from the mansion? That's a little spooky, ain't it?"

Natalie shook her head. "I don't believe in all that, and you know it."

"In all what?" Margaret played dumb enjoying the aggravation she was creating in her friend.

"Ghosts and witches and all that crazy stuff."

Margaret leaned back with surprise. "Who said anything about witches? But, since you mentioned it, I also heard that Liz Bradford had dabbled in the occult. One of her friends told another waitress at The Rex Plaza that she promised to curse Devon from the grave if he ever hurt her again."

Natalie shook her head with amusement. "Where do you get all your information?"

Margaret shrugged then reached for Natalie's hand. She took a deep breath and stared into Natalie's eyes like a mother desperate and fearful for her child. She had to make Natalie aware of the danger facing her.

"Listen to me. Lindenwood is haunted, girl. That woman was murdered in cold blood. This ain't secret news. It's all over town."

✝

CHAPTER 15

Natalie stood in front of the floor length mirror examining her reflection like an anorexic agonizing over a pound of gained weight. Nothing looked right on her. She felt ugly. She sighed heavily and smoothed the lipstick across her lips. As she turned to inspect her hair one last time, a knock came at the front door.

Devon Bradford stood on the porch waiting for Natalie. He had dinner planned at Lindenwood for the two of them. The table was set with fine linen and china, waiting on them in the soft candlelight of the upstairs dining room. Devon wore a pair of light beige trousers and alligator skin loafers. His ivory shirt was starched and tucked neatly in. Devon's style was unlike any Natalie had known before. The fancy clothes and promiscuous way he spent his money charmed her like magic. It was all a part of his plan. Before long, Natalie Houston would be right where he wanted her, at

Lindenwood taking care of his children while he waited for his upcoming trial. He needed someone like her on his side. And she was perfect, vulnerable and gullible like an infant straight from the womb.

Natalie started for the front door, her heart beating quickly. She couldn't wait to see Devon and his home. She reached for the knob and opened the door to find Devon smiling appreciatively as his eyes roamed the length of her body. He made her feel beautiful in spite of what she thought of herself.

Devon reached for Natalie's hand. He placed his lips on her hand and pulled her closer to him. He gazed into her eyes. "Hey, pretty lady. I have a surprise for you."

Devon walked Natalie to the car and opened the passenger side door of the Lincoln. As she got in, she glanced all around the rich, leather interior of the car. She felt privileged to be with him. Any woman could surely have Devon Bradford, and he had chosen her.

Devon drove steadfast to his goal. He wanted to get Natalie in the right atmosphere before he proposed. He knew she would probably hesitate to say 'yes' because of her divorce only a few months ago, but he also knew how to charm her. How could anyone say no to a life with him at Lindenwood, especially someone who had never known such security?

Natalie listened to the soft sounds of *Love Me Tender* coming from the radio. She fantasized about a life with Devon, a romantic husband who would be financially able to treat her like she had always longed to be treated. He would be a caring father, someone who wanted to be a part of her children's lives. Maybe there was some truth in the old saying, "Third time is the charm". Natalie chewed her bottom lip. She wanted to believe everything he said, all the stories of his life with Liz Bradford. How all he ever wanted was a devoted mother and wife. But, what if he asked her to marry him? Natalie felt a sweep of joy and uncertainty as she toyed with the idea. What would her family think? They had not dated very long.

Devon drove several miles down Highway 35 before they reached the mansion's drive. A small country store faced the house from the other side of the highway. Natalie noticed the old gas pumps in front of the store and the empty crates of Coca-Cola bottles stacked by the front door.

"This is it." Devon regained Natalie's attention. He drove up the long, paved drive and parked under the overhead balcony.

Natalie admired the lot covered in trees. Tall Pine trees and Oaks towered over the house. The lawn was landscaped with care, each shrub being pruned without a stray limb peeking through. The Crepe Myrtles painted the front of the house with pink, purple, and white blooms.

Devon led Natalie to the back door of the house. He put his key into the lock and twisted the knob, pushing it open. He motioned for her to go in.

Natalie's mouth hung open as she entered the back part of the mansion. Just as she stepped inside the back door, she noticed a hair salon on the left. She peeked through the door of the room. Sunlight beamed through the back window casting light into the darkness. Hair rollers and styling tools still lined the counter of Liz Bradford's salon now being occupied by James Bradford. Posters of bikini-clad women lined the walls along with posters of wild animals that glowed under black lights. The former salon had little furniture other than a stereo system, chest of drawers, and a bed with linens strewn about.

Natalie continued down the hall and through another living area before she reached the main entrance to the mansion. The house seemed to take on an atmosphere of grandeur as she entered the great room. Black leather furniture accented the red shag carpet and the black candelabras that hung on the wall. A giant iron chandelier was suspended in the middle of the room. With the area being wide open, Natalie could see there were six bedrooms on the second floor and a large kitchen with a dining area. The house was dark but impressive with elegant wall coverings laced with raised velvet patterns.

Devon stood still, watching Natalie's reaction. He was pleased. The look of desire on Natalie's face was all he needed to affirm her weakness for money. He leaned over and put his arm around her. "I've got some red wine upstairs."

Natalie smiled and leaned in to kiss Devon. She started for the stairs and stopped abruptly as she felt a sudden rush of icy, cold air. She rubbed her arms and looked at Devon, her eyes seeking an explanation.

"Did you feel that?"

"What, that cold air? Yeah, it's just the air vents from above. This house plan is wide open and sometimes the air doesn't circulate well." Devon ignored her and climbed the stairs.

Natalie looked around the room. The house was too dark for her liking. It seemed almost angry and depressed. The two front windows looked like a row of vertical eyes peering out across the highway to the gravesite. She wondered why Devon hadn't installed more lights in the house. She hurried upstairs where Devon was waiting to seat her. The table glowed under the candlelight. "This is beautiful, Devon. Everything looks so delicious." Natalie laid her napkin across her lap as she sat down.

"All for you, love." Devon poured wine in both of the thick, crystal stems. He lifted his glass and gestured for a toast. "Here's to us. What's mine is yours."

Natalie almost choked. She glanced out of the corner of her eyes. She immediately started to eat. She was nervous. What did he mean?

"Aren't you going to eat?" She asked as she placed a piece of meat between her lips and moaned in appreciation of the taste.

Devon rested his elbows on the table with his hands clasped together. "I can't. I'm too excited."

Natalie shook her head in amusement. "About what? Surely, my company isn't that overwhelming."

"I don't want your company, Natalie. I want your life. With me, here at Lindenwood."

Natalie felt her face flushing with heat, a tingling feeling creeping up her back. Her dream lover was going to ask her to marry him. It was really happening. She put her fork down, and suddenly turned serious.

"Devon, you know about my two failed marriages. I don't want another."

He reached for her hand and rubbed it between his. "You won't have another failed marriage, but you *will* have a life like you've never known."

Tears began to flood Natalie's eyes. She fought to keep them back.

"Devon, I want to believe you. But, I will not put my children through another ordeal. I can't."

"Then, believe me. I need you. Call it a marriage proposal or call it a business contract, but marry me."

Natalie gazed deeply at Devon. The touch of his hand sent ripples of pleasure over her body. The intensity of his blue eyes seared her soul. She noticed the way he studied her face, watching her expressions and paying special attention to her eyes. She felt as if he had cast a spell over her, but it was a spell she didn't want broken. Devon needed her, and he promised her a better life. Could this really be happening to her? Was she finally getting a break? Meeting the right man with all parts of the fairytale in place?

Natalie nodded. She rubbed her shoulders again as the same brush of icy, cold air swept past her. This time she looked past Devon Bradford as she heard glass splintering in the kitchen. Natalie stared around the room searching for the eyes she felt raking over her. She saw no one, but she felt the presence of something sinister and foreboding. She sighed and turned her attention back to Devon. Margaret's tales were causing her to be paranoid. Why did she even listen to her?

Devon stood beside Natalie. His mouth was in a wide smile that screamed the contentment that he felt. He had won. And without much effort, he had charmed Natalie Houston into his lair. He placed his arms around his new bride-to-be.

"Welcome to Lindenwood." He held her head close to his chest. His smile began to be replaced with a look of twisted satisfaction. His eyes glared absently around the room surrounded by the venomous spirit of Liz Bradford who swirled her icy, cold presence closer and closer to the happy couple.

✝

CHAPTER 16

Four days had passed since Natalie had talked to Devon. He had told her he was going out of town on business and wouldn't be back until the weekend. What she didn't know was that he was traveling across state lines. She never second-guessed where his money came from. Questions without answers meant she didn't have to accept reality. Her fantasy might end if she knew the truth.

She sat at the hospital desk recording vital signs in medical charts. A teenage boy wearing a red baseball cap stopped at the desk. Natalie looked up to see him carrying an arrangement of flowers. He sat the basket on the counter above her. The fresh scent of roses filled the air. Twelve red roses surrounded by violets and baby's breath were arranged in a basket. Greenery accented the design glistening with beads of moisture.

"May I help you?" Natalie noticed the boy's stained and dirty fingertips. He placed the arrangement on the counter.

"Yes. I have a delivery for Natalie Houston." He looked around the desk as if he was searching for his customer.

"That's me." She dropped her pen on the desk and stared at the flowers, stunned by the surprise. She twirled the basket around and untied the ribbon holding the envelope as she ripped the paper away.

Inside was a plain white card. It read,

"I do."
Devon,

The words took her breath, goose bumps covered her body. Devon was such a romantic. How could she have ever doubted his love? She held the note close to her chest. She and Devon were going to be married in just a matter of weeks. The only thing that might kill the fairytale was if Devon was proven guilty in his next trial. Natalie would be there. Not only was Devon's life dangling by the jury's decision, but Natalie Bradford's future could be significantly altered either way.

Devon insisted that she begin moving her things to Lindenwood, but Natalie refused to stay in the mansion overnight. She didn't feel safe when he had to leave for work late at night. The invisible eyes were everywhere she went in the house, never leaving her side. She wasn't prepared to confront the spirit of Liz Bradford since she didn't believe in ghosts. She believed in intuition, the innate power all humans possess that acts like an internal compass, but her failure to trust it lay within her understanding of its mystery and ability to detect spiritual frequencies naked to the human eye. Margaret York stood in the doorway of the break room, observing Natalie's reaction.

"Hey, Girl. What is this?" Margaret winked at Natalie and pointed to the basket as she walked over to the counter.

"It's from Devon." Natalie purred loudly

Margaret opened the card and read the note.

"My! My! Isn't he a charmer?" Her tone was sarcastic.

Natalie noticed Margaret's sharpness and frowned. She had been avoiding Margaret. She believed that Margaret had lied to her about Devon. She wondered why people couldn't just be happy for her. Why was everyone always against her?

Margaret was afraid Natalie would turn cold, but she felt she had to tell her. If he were as cunning and sly as she had heard, Natalie would figure him out sooner than later. Even though Natalie often found herself with the wrong man, she was also known to be smart and suspicious. Margaret believed that Natalie's true fault was her inability to be alone.

"Margaret-

Margaret turned to face Natalie. She brushed a blond strand away from her slender face. She stood with one foot crossed over the other waiting for Natalie to continue.

"I- I guess I need to tell you this since you're going to have to buy a dress."

Margaret grabbed her mouth. "What? You're kidding."

Natalie shook her head, and jumped two inches off the floor. She grabbed Margaret, eager to receive her friend's good wishes.

"Nope, it's true. I'm moving to Lindenwood as Mrs. Devon Bradford."

"When?" Margaret's eyes were wide with disbelief.

"August 5th. He wants to get married soon, Marg. Can you believe this is happening? A rich, gorgeous man wants to marry me!"

Margaret shook her head. She couldn't believe Natalie Houston was utterly spellbound by a man she barely knew. She leaned forward and hugged her friend, closing her eyes in fear of what was to come.

Only one person knew that Natalie was getting married on the same day Liz Bradford would have been forty-one years old. Nobody knew, but Devon Bradford himself. It was his choice. In his sick way of having the last word, he wanted a new Liz Bradford for Lindenwood. And he picked his deceased wife's birthday as the day when Natalie Houston would be re-born into the role he had planned.

Signs were all around Natalie Bradford. Signs were screaming 'BEWARE", but she couldn't see them. Denial was easier than facing a possible truth about her lover, and in five short days, her fate would be sealed by a detective's undisclosed exhibit.

CHAPTER 17

Devon Bradford walked assuredly into the same courtroom that had delivered his guilty verdict two years earlier. He had finally gotten a new trial after his appeal to the Mississippi State Supreme Court. On June 13th, 1975, Devon was found guilty of manslaughter. Now it was the exact same day two years later that he would be beginning a new trial and his last hope at freedom.

Bill Russell adjusted the waist of his pants, pulling them higher across his waist as he readied himself for another courtroom drama. A few things had changed since the first trial and he was confident that the D.A. didn't have a chance. All of the evidence was circumstantial and once again there were no witnesses. Natalie Houston sat in the courtroom audience. She attempted to soothe the tension in her hands as she massaged her palms. She was fearful for Devon. What would become of him? Would their dreams be shattered if he was found guilty?

Bill Russell walked over to the jury and casually leaned against the ledge separating him from the jury box. He pulled at his pants and addressed the jury with a stern look and tone.

"Ladies and Gentlemen, you've heard this case. You have seen the evidence or rather the lack of evidence that proves beyond a shadow of a doubt that Mr. Devon Bradford murdered his wife. You've even seen the incompetency of the Tupelo Police Department's care in securing state's evidence. The detective never even sent the crime weapon or Mrs. Bradford's hair samples to the state crime lab. We know that these items stayed locked inside his desk drawer at the police department. But, can we testify that this evidence was never altered or tampered with? Can we say without any doubt that this evidence the D.A. believes proves Devon Bradford is a killer is 100% without error? No, we cannot, and because of this, you absolutely must return a verdict of not guilty in this case."

George Dennis knew there was no point in disputing Russell's closing argument. The verdict had been overturned by faulty detective work. Why had Detective Wilson failed to secure state's evidence and follow proper procedure? Was he that careless in his job or did he have some other motive? Didn't he know the importance of sending evidence to the state crime lab in Jackson? None of it mattered now. If Devon Bradford was a killer, he was about to be a free one.

Judge Whitt ordered a recess before court was to reconvene for the verdict reading. It didn't take the jury long to know what they had to do.

The courtroom was silent as everyone waited. The tensions Natalie and Devon had felt were slowly subsiding. Devon had a look of smug satisfaction that he kept hidden until now. He quietly contemplated his next move with Natalie. He could now set a date for marriage. His life would be restored to him.

"All rise." The bailiff's order brought everyone to attention as the judge entered the bench. Everyone in the courtroom seemed to study the juror's faces.

"Madam Juror, have you reached a verdict?"

"We have, Your Honor."

The bailiff stepped forward ready to pass the verdict to the judge.

"Go ahead, please." Judge Whitt waited.

"We, the jury, find the defendant, Devon Bradford, not guilty on all counts."

A wave of relief swept over Natalie and Devon. Whispers of congratulations and other's grievances filled the courtroom as the crowd cleared out. Later, there would be a party celebrating Devon's freedom, but hidden beneath the joy lay Liz Bradford's agonizing lament. Devon's freedom meant that her killer was still unknown, and another trial was about to begin. The new trial would be starring none other than Natalie Houston. She would be the instrument Liz Bradford needed to identify her killer.

✝

CHAPTER 18

Mrs. Devon Bradford stood in the kitchen she now claimed as hers, busy washing dinner dishes and planning the children's lunches for the following day. The television played loudly downstairs with no one there to watch it. Natalie peered over the black, iron banister. She hurried down the stairs to turn the set off when the screen abruptly changed to a news alert.

The news anchor spoke with urgency.

"We have just gotten news that Elvis Presley is dead. He was found dead in his Graceland home." The reporter looked grief stricken.

Natalie's hand went to her mouth as tears began to pour from her eyes. Her sobs became louder echoing throughout the great room. Anna and Audrey heard her cries and came out of their rooms.

"What's wrong, Mama?" Anna rushed down the stairs, staring at the television.

Natalie pointed to the television. "Elvis is dead. I can't believe it. Elvis is really dead." She shook her head.

Anna walked over to the television and looked at the screen. Thousands of mourners lined the street outside Graceland. Anna's eyes began to water at the sight of others tormented over the loss. She turned to leave the room, not wanting to cry in front of her new stepsister. She started back up the stairs when she heard a slamming noise coming from the kitchen.

Natalie looked confused as she wiped the tears from her face. "What was that?" She started for the stairs as the noise became louder like a blast.

"I don't know. It sounds like the cabinet doors are being ripped off!"

Natalie shouted toward the kitchen. "Hey! What's going on up there?"

She skipped a step as she climbed the staircase. When she reached the top of the stairs, the noise fell dead quiet. A chilling calmness settled over the kitchen without reason.

Natalie shivered. "Why is this house so cold all the time?" She rubbed her neck as the chill crept up her back. She started for the stairs, anxious to get back to the news of Elvis's death.

"What was that noise, Mama?" Anna's brownish blonde hair hung in wavy strands of curls below her shoulders, her green eyes wide with wonder.

"Oh, it was probably just some pots and pans shifting in the cabinet." Natalie didn't believe it was pots and pans shifting in the cabinets, but neither did she believe a ghost was causing the noise. She wasn't going to fall for Margaret's jokes. There had to be a logical explanation.

Anna felt the urge to hide. She didn't believe pots and pans could make noises that loud. She stared over her shoulder as she ran for the hall leading to her bedroom. She didn't like the feeling of being scared all the time, and since they had moved to Lindenwood she could never shake her uneasy feelings. Even when she was alone, she felt as if someone was watching her and waiting. But waiting for what? She had heard other children talk about haunted houses, but she never dreamed that she would be living in one.

Rebecca Bradford, now a budding young woman at sixteen years of age, watched Anna run to her room. She walked around the side of the banister and stood in the doorway to Anna's room. Anna busied herself unpacking dolls.

"This used to be my room when Mama was alive. I got to pick out my own carpet." Rebecca said with pride.

"Oh, I like it. Purple is my mama's favorite color." Rebecca nodded as if she knew that already. "Who is staying in Caroline's room?" She turned and pointed down the hall to the room joining Anna's. Only a bathroom separated the two rooms. The corner room was empty and the door was closed. The dead girl's memory was all that remained inside.

"Who is Caroline?" Anna asked with interest. She thought she had already met all of Devon's children.

"She is my sister, but she's dead. That was her room before she died."

"What happened to her?" Anna's little girl voice was filled with curiosity.

"She drowned with her boyfriend at the park."

"What grade was she in?" Anna stopped unpacking her dolls and turned to look at Rebecca.

"She was only in the 9th grade. She was fourteen." Rebecca sat down on the edge of Anna's bed.

Anna rubbed the fur on a stuffed polar bear that Devon had given her. She looked at the bear and remembered how Devon had cheated at the dime toss game when he won it for her.

"Would you like to see some pictures? I've got some I can show you of my mom and sister." Rebecca motioned for Anna to follow her.

"Okay." Anna toted the bear with her.

They ran to the stairs skipping a step until they reached the bottom. Rebecca led Anna into the den where she pulled a box from a closet under the stairs. The box was hidden with a quilt covering the secret closet. She pulled back the quilt and began to lift handfuls of pictures and dusty, worn books collected by Liz Bradford.

"Do you wanna know a secret?" Rebecca asked as she knelt on one knee.

"Yeah." Anna whispered with excitement.

"My mom was a witch."

Anna gasped. Her skin tingled. "Really?"

Rebecca nodded firmly. She held up a tattered and torn book before Anna's face. The pages were blue and the cover smelled of mildew. She opened the book to the first chapter and pointed to the page in front of her.

"Yeah, really. And she still is."

✝

CHAPTER 19

Anna turned her eyes away from Rebecca, not sure what to say. The two girls dug through the box of pictures. Rebecca found two pictures and handed them to Anna. Anna studied the pictures of Caroline Bradford and her dead mother. Caroline had an uncanny resemblance to Audrey, except for her blue eyes. Her skin was an olive tone, smooth and youthful, and her hair was dark brown.

The other picture brought forth an unnerving silence. Dressed in blue, Liz Bradford lay still surrounded by ruffles of white satin that lined the coffin. Her hair looked dry and brittle. Bruises were evident about her neck and the funeral home had been unsuccessful in hiding the bullet wounds to her head. Although her hair had been carefully styled, it was not long enough to cover the entry hole behind her left ear.

Anna gazed at the deceased body. The hair at the back of her neck began to rise, and she felt her skin crawling with goose bumps. The reality of the photo was too much. Even as a young eight year old, she sensed that Liz Bradford was probably angry when she died. She began to envision Liz Bradford opening her eyes and rising from the coffin to get revenge on her killer. Anna abruptly handed the picture back to Rebecca.

Unknowing to both of them, Timothy Houston was eavesdropping behind the door. He jumped out with his arms in the air.

"Run!" He shouted, slinging his arms in the air.

Rebecca and Anna screamed. Tears swelled up in Anna's eyes.

"You idiot! Don't ever do that again." Rebecca demanded. Timothy laughed loudly. He was a hyper kid of twelve years. He needed constant stimulation in order to be happy. Most of the time he sought creative pursuits through art and music, but if he got bored, Anna was usually an easy target. His dark brown wavy hair and brown eyes were the exact image of his father's German heritage.

"I was just playing around. What are y'all up to?" Timothy casually joined in without an invitation.

"We were looking at some pictures until you scared us to death." Anna glared at her brother.

"I wanna see. Show me." Timothy sat down on the floor beside Rebecca. She handed him the pictures of her mother.

"Your mom wasn't a witch." Timothy said

arguing.

"Oh, yes, she was. Her books are in this box." Rebecca pointed to the box at her feet. "But, listen, you guys can't tell anyone what I just told you."

"That's a bunch of bull." Timothy looked at Rebecca like she was stupid.

"Whatever, Timothy. Just don't tell. Alright?" Rebecca said with frustration.

Rebecca glared at Timothy. She put her hands on his arms and forced him to look her in the face. "Listen, Timothy. My mother cursed my dad for killing her. And her spirit won't rest until he pays for what he did."

"Okay, okay." Timothy began to feel uncomfortable. He shook his arms free and picked up the picture of Caroline Bradford. As his eyes gazed at her image, dozens of questions raced through his mind. Her long dark brown hair draped over her thin shoulders. She stood tall on the back row of her fellow teammates on the basketball team. Her smile was shy suggesting a quiet nature while her pale blue eyes burned into his mind.

"Didn't she drown?" Timothy asked with curiosity.

"Uh, huh. She was with her boyfriend. He drowned, too."

"What happened?" Timothy was now eager to hear the story and at the same time felt eerie about claiming her old room.

"They fell out of a boat."

"How old was she?"

"Fourteen. She died a year or so before mama."

"Oh." Timothy felt awkward.

"Hey, their graves are across the highway on the hill. You can see them from upstairs. Come on, and I'll show you."

Rebecca jumped up motioning for Timothy and Anna to follow. They ran up the stairs and around the banister in front of Anna's room. Rebecca stopped and pointed out the front window.

"See, there's the tombstones, and at night it gets real foggy over there."

Timothy stared out the window. Two tombstones stood alone at the far side of the cemetery. The hill overlooked the mansion. Both graves had a small arrangement of plastic flowers at the base of the graves.

Anna began backing away from the two of them, her expression full of fear. Visions of the two deceased women rushed through her mind. She felt emotions that weren't her own. It was as if she was reading the dead women's mind and experiencing their feelings from another time. Anna was too young to understand her ability to see the past much less the future. It was uncomfortable for her and frightening. She raced down the stairs to find Natalie folding laundry in the master suite. She rushed through the door and flopped down on the corner of the bed.

"What are you doing, Anna?" Natalie looked at her daughter with suspicion.

"I don't know. Nothing." Anna sheepishly replied. She waited a moment before deciding to tell her mother about the witch.

"I don't like it upstairs, Mama. It's too dark."

"You'll be okay. Your brother is going to be right next door to you."

"But, I'm scared. Can I sleep with you?"

"No, Anna. Devon will be sleeping with me. What's wrong with you?" Natalie stopped folding clothes and looked at her daughter with irritation.

"Why don't you want to sleep in your room?"

Anna stared at the floor. "There's a ghost up there."

"There is not." Natalie's hands rested on her hips.

"Yes, there is, and Rebecca's mama was a witch." Anna was breathless.

"Who told you that?"

"Rebecca did, but I saw the books."

"That's enough of that. Now go upstairs and get ready for bed. You need to get your bathwater ready." Natalie shook her head. She mumbled to herself. Her kids had such vivid imaginations.

Anna took her time leaving the safety of her mother's room. She cautiously walked up the stairs looking all around as she went. Timothy and Rebecca had disappeared to their rooms leaving her alone. She went into her bathroom and turned the tub faucet on. The water rushed into the tub, filling it quickly.

She stared at the bathroom door that led to Caroline's old room. The distinct odor of mothballs tickled her nose as visions of Caroline raced through her mind. She quickly stepped out of her clothes and got into the warm water. She washed herself faster than she ever had.

Anna looked above her head and all around the room. She jerked around and inspected the window above the tub. She felt the unseen eyes of someone watching her, studying her with the curiousness of a cat exploring its prey. She placed her arms across her chest in an effort to shield her nakedness and hastily got out of the tub, her eyes never leaving the door that joined her bathroom to the dead girl's bedroom.

CHAPTER 20

Two hours later, Timothy began to drift off to sleep. He had finished settling into Caroline's old room and had left the door slightly open before he climbed into bed. The bathroom door leading to Anna's room was closed.

Anna lay asleep for over an hour. Her full size bed was piled high with stuffed animals. She had stared at the ceiling, counting sheep and saying her prayers for protection from what she couldn't see. She knew little about the paranormal world. Her education of ghosts had only been through movies and kid's books, but she had the discernment of a child, susceptible to ghostly phenomenon. And she knew when something wasn't right.

A sweet odor of perfume began to drift about the small corner bedroom where Timothy lay. He began to toss and turn, unconsciously burying his face in his pillow. The light switch near the door clicked on. Timothy stirred as he heard the whispers of his name. He didn't recognize the voice, but the urgency in the girl's plea startled him. He jerked awake and sat up in bed. His eyes were squinted from the glare of the overhead light. He jumped out of bed and flicked the switch off. As he lay awake staring in the darkness, he wondered who had turned the light on. Or, had he fallen asleep with it on? Finally his eyelids became too heavy to keep open, and he drifted back to sleep.

At seven a.m., the sun beaming through the window awoke Timothy. He rolled out of bed and wandered sleepily to the kitchen. Audrey and Anna sat at the bar eating cereal. Timothy watched Anna chomping on the cereal, her upper lip soaked with milk. She attempted to ignore him, but gave him a scowl as he stared. She thought he was acting weirder than usual.

"Anna, why did you turn the light on in my room last night?" Timothy stood next to Anna, his hands placed in front of her on the bar.

"I didn't." Anna stopped eating and stared blankly at Timothy.

"Yes, you did. I woke up, and it was on."

"I did not!" Anna shouted. Her voice echoed throughout the top floor.

Natalie heard the commotion from the bottom of the stairs. She quickly climbed the stairs. "What is going on up here?"

"Anna came in my room last night nosing around and left my light on."

"No, I didn't, Mama. I was asleep." She shook her head and picked up her spoon.

"Maybe you left the light on, Timothy. Just check yourself tonight. Now, hurry up and eat. You're gonna miss the school bus."

Timothy poured a bowl of cereal and sat at the end of the bar by himself. He gulped his food down and hurriedly returned to his room to get dressed. As he walked through the door, he noticed everything was just as he left it. He wondered if he was having a bad dream the night before. He stood by the bed and looked around the small cramped space. A chest of drawers sat flush against a wall under a high window. The walls were made of a white colored paneling, and the carpet was thick, navy blue shag. His small twin size bed rested against a wall just inside the door. He grabbed his schoolbooks scattered about the floor and headed out the door. He had no way of knowing who he would be meeting just hours later in a nocturnal nightmare that would transform itself into reality. Yes, she was coming.

†

CHAPTER 21

The moon illuminated Lindenwood casting shadows across the mansion's rooftop. The interior of the mansion was cool in spite of the roaring fires that burned in the home's two chimneys. Across the street, the graves of Liz and Caroline Bradford seemed to glow as an eerie fog stood suspended a few feet above the earth.

Timothy packed his trumpet back in its case and lazily walked toward the stairs. He wiped his eyes and thought about the last night's dreams. The upstairs was dim with only a yellow glow lighting the path to Caroline Bradford's old room. The house was quiescent. The other children had turned in for the night. Downstairs, Natalie began preparing for bed as she applied moisturizer to her face. A small television played in the background. Flickers of light and muffled voices seeped from under the closed door.

Timothy stepped closer toward his bedroom and stopped dead still. He froze as he stared through the open door into the darkness. Nothing looked odd, but he felt uneasy. He cautiously approached the room and reached in, flicking on the light. He panicked and ran for the bed. He leaped in mid-air, landing in the middle of the bed as it shook and bounced.

He crawled quickly under the sheets and lay motionless. He took a deep breath and tried to relax his body. His breathing was heavy until he became exhausted from dread. As his eyelids closed, Timothy was unaware of the temperature changing in Caroline's room. A fog lingered over his mouth with every breath. He shivered in his sleep. The lights began to flicker, this time clicking on and off simultaneously.

"Timothy, help me." Whispers gently tickled his ear. Then, without warning a voice screamed in horror. "Timothy, save me!"

Timothy bolted straight up in his bed gasping for breath. His eyes were wide as his body shook. He searched the empty room. The light above was burning bright. He crawled out of bed, dragging a blanket and pillow with him. No one would believe him if he told anyone that Caroline Bradford was calling his name from the grave.

Timothy dashed out of the room. He turned his head toward the wall, refusing to look in the direction of Caroline's grave. He ran down the stairs, skipping a step as he went and settled on the sofa outside the master suite.

Natalie woke at her usual 6:30 a.m. She went about her usual morning routine, showering off before going upstairs for coffee. Timothy snored underneath the blankets covering his head. He had a strange way of rolling himself up like a mummy while he slept. Natalie opened the bedroom door. She stopped as soon as she saw Timothy sleeping soundly on the sofa.

Natalie gently nudged Timothy's shoulder. "Timothy, wake up." He stretched and peeked from under the blanket. "Did you sleep here all night?"

"Uh, huh." Timothy mumbled as he cleared his voice.

"Why?" Natalie asked puzzled.

"Somebody is bothering me in my room."

"What do you mean?" Natalie knew Timothy wasn't fabricating a story.

He shook his head. "I don't know who, but the light keeps coming on, and I keep hearing voices. I don't want to stay up there anymore."

Timothy sat up and rubbed his eyes. He tried to keep from sounding like a wimp, but it was almost beyond his control. He knew he didn't want to be in that room again if Caroline Bradford decided to come back. How could he tell his mother that a ghost was visiting him every night?

Natalie looked concerned. "I'll get Devon to check your light switch today. We'll change it if we need to. You probably just aren't used to living in a new house."

Natalie offered Timothy a hand to stand and started for the upstairs. She thought about what Margaret had told her. Their conversation reeled through her mind like a spinning record. Could there be any truth behind her peculiar beliefs? If there were ghosts at Lindenwood, were they the ghosts of Liz Bradford or her deceased daughter? And, if they were there, what did they want?

CHAPTER 22

Timothy's feet brushed across the carpet in the stillness of the living room. He mounted the stairs and slowly eased up the stairs. His head ached from lack of sleep and worry. He found it difficult to concentrate in class as the sounds of Caroline's whisper lingered in his ears. He walked through the bedroom door and reached for the light switch. The switch had been replaced with a dimmer knob. He examined the switch plate and toyed with the light turning it up and down. As he threw his schoolbooks in the corner, Natalie appeared in the doorway.

"You shouldn't have any more trouble with these lights." She leaned against the doorframe and searched Timothy's face for approval.

"Man, I hope not." Timothy shook his head and climbed into bed. He felt silly telling his mother that he heard a ghost. He didn't want anyone to know. They might think he was a sissy.

Natalie pushed the switch off. "Goodnight, Timothy. Call me if you need anything." Her voice was calm and sincere.

"I'll be fine, Mama." Timothy said with irritation. He motioned for Natalie to go away. She was treating him like a child. He didn't need to be tucked in. He was not a baby anymore. He listened as her footsteps echoed on the stairs, squeaking every other step.

Everyone else was already asleep at Lindenwood. The mansion seemed tranquil in the silence. The upstairs hall light glowed, lighting a dim path to Timothy's door. No one was disturbed until the footsteps began to ascend the staircase.

Timothy turned on his left side facing the wall. He pulled the blanket over his head and began to mumble to himself as he counted sheep for the third night. He watched the stars through the window above his bed mouthing the numbers to himself.

"Thirty-five, thirty-six, thirty-." Timothy's lips became quiet. His mouth remained slightly open as his eyes closed.

The stairs squeaked and cracked. Once again the temperature on the top floor began to drop below fifty degrees. Heavy scents of Jasmine perfume escaped from beyond Timothy's door. The whispering began to fill Caroline's old room becoming louder as Timothy lay sleeping.

"Timothy! Help me." Faint screams from a distant caused Timothy to stir. He tossed from one side to another. He heard water splashing. Beams of moonlight lit up his room as he slowly peeked from behind the blanket. Where was the water coming from?

The voice came again. Timothy froze. He felt paralyzed. He couldn't feel himself breathing, his body rigid with fear. His breath created a fog with each exhale. His eyes filled with tears. He squeezed his eyes shut and prayed.

"Please make it go away, God."

Without warning a piercing scream rang throughout the room. Timothy's head jerked as he grabbed the blankets and threw them off his body. His body was overcome with convulsions as he beheld the spirit of Caroline Bradford standing at the foot of his bed, repeatedly calling out to him. Her hair was just as he remembered in her picture, long and shiny black with her eyes almost translucent blue, but her skin was dull and lifeless in the morbid image of decay.

Timothy struggled to breathe. Tears poured over his eyelids as he flung himself onto the floor and crawled under the bed. He gasped and coughed trying to catch his breath. Suddenly he felt relief as he heard Anna's familiar footsteps.

"Timothy? Are you okay?" She pushed the door open.

Timothy wiped his face and began to crawl from under the bed.

"What are you doing under the bed? I thought I heard you fall."

"I thought I saw something, but it's gone now. I don't want to sleep in this room anymore." Timothy was shaking. He picked up a blanket from the floor and pulled it tight around his body.

"Gosh, it's cold in here." Anna shivered.

"I know. Come on. Let's go get in your bed." Timothy moved quickly past Anna.

She looked at him sleepy-eyed and followed him to her room. She climbed into bed and settled under the covers. She wondered why her brother was under the bed shaking uncontrollably. She had never seen him that scared before. She stared at the ceiling and thought about the 'eyes' in her bathroom. What if they were watching him too?

"What did you see, Timothy?" Anna whispered in the dark. She was overcome with curiosity in spite of her fear.

Timothy put his finger to his lips.

"Sh-h-h. She might come back."

✝

CHAPTER 23

The Saturday morning sun woke Natalie from a peaceful slumber. She rolled over and glanced at the clock on the bedside table. It was 6:30 a.m., and Devon wasn't home. She rubbed her face and coughed, clearing her dry throat. She threw her legs over the side of the bed and sat still looking around the room. Devon had been coming home late for the past two weeks. Natalie wasn't sure how she should approach him, but she was tired of not knowing her new husband's whereabouts.

Natalie slipped a T-shirt over her head and pulled her shoulder length hair back in a ponytail. She grabbed a pair of faded jeans and slip-on sandals before searching for her car keys and a piece of paper to leave Devon a note.

Natalie quietly closed the back door trying not to wake any of the children. She noticed that Anna's door was partially closed as she passed through the living room and thought it was rather peculiar knowing her daughter always slept with the door open.

Natalie cranked the Oldsmobile. The gas gauge registered a half tank of fuel. Natalie frowned with aggravation.

"That's weird. I know I just filled this car up two days ago." She said aloud. She glanced down to check her mileage odometer. She always cleared the trip meter to zero after filling up with gas. The odometer read 65,033 miles with 251 miles driven since the fill-up.

"This can't be right. I haven't driven this car 250 miles in 2 days." Natalie played with the odometer stem pushing it back and forth as the numbers flashed. Who had driven her car?

She put the car in reverse and backed down the long gravel driveway. As she pulled out into the highway, she chewed on her middle fingernail and pondered over the mysterious extra mileage on her car. Someone had to have driven her car during the night when she was asleep, but who and why? Devon wasn't home. He had been at work. Who would want to use her car?

Natalie turned into the parking lot of the old country store. She walked in and stood in front of the donut case waiting for the store clerk to help her with a selection. The building smelled of melted sugar and glaze, and the sweet aroma of baked donuts filled her nose. Her mouth watered.

"Good mornin." The clerk's eyes looked tired and her short dark brown hair had two splotches of flour among the tousled mess. Her twelve-hour shift had gone over by thirty minutes.

"Mornin. I'll have two dozen of the glazed donuts, please." Natalie watched her as she carefully packed the boxes.

The clerk studied Natalie through the glass counter. She had seen her somewhere before. She was sure of it, but she couldn't decide where.

"You look so familiar to me. Do you live around here?" The clerk's voice was full of curiosity even though she tried not to sound obvious.

"Yeah, I live in the Lindenwood house."

The clerk's mouth fell open. She dropped one of the donuts on the floor as she stood with a look of surprise. She hoped Natalie had not noticed.

"Oh, I know who you remind me of. You look like the lady that used to live there."

Natalie felt her skin tingle. "Oh, really?"

"Yeah, you resemble her. Are you the new Mrs. Bradford?" She pretended to be half-interested as she finished filling the box.

Natalie nodded. She didn't speak, but stood quiet. She was stunned to hear that she looked like Devon's deceased wife.

"You know, I knew Liz Bradford for a short time. She used to come to my church. She always brought the children, but I never saw her husband with her. I hope the kids are doing well." She smiled at Natalie through the glass.

"They're doin' fine." Natalie squeezed her hands together. She was nervous, but couldn't help wondering what the woman knew.

"Well, I'm so glad to hear that. Bless their hearts. They've been through so much with their mother being murdered and all." The clerk continued packing donuts never looking up.

"Murdered?" Natalie played dumb.

The clerk stopped and looked at Natalie with caution.

"You don't know the story of Liz Bradford? It's a million wonders her soul can rest."

"No, I guess I don't. When did that happen?" Natalie waited for more information, but the clerk's hands began to tremble. She quickly finished packaging Natalie's order.

"About two years ago. I can't believe you don't know."

"Know what?" Natalie pressed.

The clerk avoided eye contact. She refused to say anything else about Liz Bradford.

"That's two dozen donuts for you. That'll be $4.59." Natalie noticed her hands shaking. The clerk bagged the boxes and handed them over the counter.

"Thank you and have a nice day." The clerk disappeared behind the counter. Natalie stood still for a moment in bewilderment. She snapped her purse shut and walked out the front door. As she made her way back to Lindenwood, she thought about the clerk's odd behavior. The clerk's sudden frightened look had unnerved her. Why did that clerk feel scared to tell her anything else?

Natalie began to get suspicious of Devon's whereabouts. She began to slow the car as she approached Marty's café, a popular spot for locals to drink coffee and talk shop. Natalie scanned the parking lot. She firmly pressed on the brakes as she spotted Devon's truck parked on the side of the café. She pulled around to the opposite side of the building and turned the car off.

Natalie got out of the car and walked like a sleuth along the sidewalk of the café. She peered through the front window and saw Devon sitting in a booth near the back of the dining room. He was reading a paper and drinking a cup of coffee. Several tables in the center of the room were occupied. A bell hanging from the door jingled as Natalie walked through the door.

"Good morning!" The cook behind the long bar lined with bar stools welcomed Natalie with a wide-toothed grin.

"Mornin." Natalie smiled back. She turned her attention to Devon who had laid his paper aside and was now staring coldly at her. His eyes followed her until she sat down across from him.

"Why are you looking at me like that?" Natalie slid down in the booth seat across from him.

"Why are you here?" Devon's voice was low and harsh. He continued to stare, puffing on his cigarette.

Devon's rejection shocked her. Her eyes moistened.

"I stopped to have a cup of coffee with you. I was on my way home from getting donuts and saw your truck here."

Devon blew smoke in Natalie's face. He laid his cigarette in the tray and returned his icy blue eyes on her. "Don't ever stop here again if I'm here. Do you understand?"

Natalie's moistened eyes began to glaze over in a green fury of her own. "What the hell is wrong with you?"

Devon stared, the demons screaming inside his head as he stared across the table at the new Liz Bradford. She had to be taught what she could and couldn't do.

"Natalie, I'm going to tell you this one time, and you'll be wise to remember it. Don't concern yourself with where I am or what I'm doing. If I want you to know, I'll tell you." He reached out and grabbed her hand. He squeezed her wrist until it turned red, his fingers burning their imprint into her flesh.

"Let go of me!" She whispered between clenched teeth. She snatched her arm away and grabbed her purse. As she stormed out the front door, tears poured over her cheeks. She was humiliated and confused. She had only been married two months, and already something wasn't right.

The door slammed behind Devon. An hour had passed since Natalie had left the café. She sat upstairs at the kitchen bar staring at the walls while she nibbled on one of the donuts she had bought.

Devon's brow was furrowed, his lips tight. He walked through the den into the living room. He glared around the room, searching for Natalie. Because of her unwelcome visit at the café, he had almost missed an important meeting. Devon noticed the light coming from the upstairs kitchen. He started up the stairs staring at the back of Natalie's head, but he only saw Liz Bradford sitting on the barstool. Natalie even sipped her coffee like his dead wife, her lips meeting the cup halfway as if she were going to spill the precious drink.

Devon considered how he should handle Natalie. She was too nosy, sneaking in his business when she shouldn't be. Her place was at home with his children and his mansion. What more could she want? She had everything she had ever dreamed of. She reminded him of his rebellious wife, a woman determined to defy him. He wouldn't have it. If Natalie Houston didn't do as she was told, he would make her wish she had.

He clenched his fist before shoving them in his pockets. He massaged the wad of money he had recently acquired. It felt good to feel the stiff folds of new bills. He felt full like a lion gloating after a tiresome kill. His selfishness consumed him as he thought about Natalie. Would she start demanding more from him?

Natalie ignored Devon as he walked around the bar to face her. She took one last sip of her coffee and began to get off the stool.

"I didn't tell you to leave." Devon placed his hand on her arm and motioned for her to sit down.

"I beg your pardon. I didn't ask." Natalie looked down at his hand resting on her forearm and then back at Devon. Her eyes warned him that she would not be intimidated. Her tone was sharp. She had no patience for any excuses he might offer to explain his sudden hostile behavior.

"I'm a very private man, Natalie, and I demand a certain degree of space. I expect you to honor that from now on." Devon's cold gaze backed his warning. He leaned in closer to her and pushed himself against her.

Natalie tried not to show fear in spite of the churning feeling in her stomach. She looked at Devon with her right eyebrow cocked, a typical habit when she was angered.

"Then maybe you'll understand when I demand an explanation into your sudden change. My kids and I have lived here over a month now, and I still can't even get grocery money out of you. What happened to the promises, Devon? Where's the life you promised, the fairytale? I want some answers." She paused and stared at Devon. He refused to move, holding her arm tighter.

"Answer me, damn it! Why are you being so cold to me? Why, Devon?" Natalie shouted. Her eyes searched his.

Devon twisted Natalie's arm behind her back. She screamed in pain as she felt her bones pop. Devon spoke through clenched teeth. The tone of his voice was deep like the darkest pits of hell.

"You listen to me. This is my house. If you want to stay here, you better get that straight. You don't ask where I am or what I do with my money. It's my money. And as far as our marriage goes-

Devon seemed to look through Natalie. "I don't give a damn how you see it." He slung her arm away. He backed away and looked at her as if he were seeing someone else. Flashes of his deceased wife darted in and out of his mind. He raked his eyes over the length of her body.

"Think of our marriage as a business arrangement, Natalie. That's all it is." He turned and left Natalie alone. Her arms hung at her sides, limp and numb. Her mouth was open in astonishment.

Devon's words were like ice pouring over the exposed paths of Natalie's body. She felt herself shudder at the thought of being married to Devon Bradford. Her mind raced. Who was this man? In only two weeks, he had taken on a persona unlike any she had ever seen. She slumped back on the barstool and buried her head in her hands, releasing the pain that filled her soul. She had missed all the warning signs in the beginning, and she now knew it.

CHAPTER 24

Anna awoke early Sunday morning. It was just past 7:00 a.m. and no one was downstairs in the den. She snuck past Natalie's door without being seen and tiptoed through the den making her way to James's room. She continued to be fascinated by the snake statue and the black lights that glowed against the black velvet posters on the walls.

Anna peeked around the door of his room. James had left the bed unmade when he went hunting earlier that morning. She eased in the room careful not to make a sound. She looked all around the room as if she were ready for someone to jump from behind a door. She picked up James's record collection and flipped through the albums. She noticed that James liked some of the same groups as Timothy. She studied the make-up that

Kiss wore on the front cover of the record album. A strange smell of incense floated about his room. As she scanned the top of the dresser searching for the cones of fruit fragranced incense, a drawer pulled slightly open caught her eye.

Anna turned her attention to a bulk of towels sticking out of one side. She started to shove the towels back into the drawer when something rolled to the other side of the drawer. As she pulled the drawer open, four syringes with needles rolled to the end of the drawer. Her hand flew to her mouth. She immediately sensed something was not right. Why would James have needles? He wasn't a doctor. She slammed the drawer shut. If James caught her in his room, she would be in deep trouble.

She rushed out the door and ran straight for Natalie's room. She wanted to tell her mother, but what if she got in trouble for snooping? She had uncovered a secret that she wasn't supposed to know about.

Natalie stood over her bed still dressed in her nightgown. She fluffed the pillows as she pulled the sheets over the bed.

"Good morning, sunshine. You're up early." Natalie looked over her shoulder at Anna.

Anna sat down on the edge of the bed, breathless from the sudden flight from James's room. She chewed her thumbnail in contemplation of how she was going to tell her mother about the needles.

"Anna, has Timothy been sleeping with you in your room?" Natalie knew Anna would tell her the truth especially if it concerned Timothy. She couldn't keep a secret regardless of the consequences.

"Uh-huh." Anna swung her legs over the side of the bed.

"Why hasn't he been sleeping in his own room?"

Anna shrugged her shoulders, then turned around and faced Natalie. "Caroline scared him real bad, and he can't go back in there."

"Caroline who?" Natalie stopped and stared at Anna, her eyes full of wonder.

"You know, Audrey's sister that died. She was standing at the end of Timothy's bed."

A chill rushed over Natalie's body. She would have to talk to Timothy as soon as possible. She was worried about him. He was a nervous kid. She turned and continued straightening the room not wanting to ask any further questions.

"Mama, is James sick?" Anna swept her foot across the carpet, swinging it in front of the other one.

"Sick? I don't guess so. Why?"

"Well, I saw some needles in his room like they use at the doctor."

Natalie's eyes widened. She whirled around to face her daughter.

"Anna, don't go back in James's room ever again. Do you understand?

Anna dropped her eyes. "I'm sorry. I didn't –

"It doesn't matter. Just do as I say. If I catch you in there again, I'll spank you. Do you understand?" Natalie's hands shook.

Natalie's stomach suddenly felt sour. She was glad Anna came to her, but what would this mean for her now? She couldn't tell Devon. He might explode if he knew that Anna had been meddling. He had already issued his warning for her to keep her distance, and now her own children were uncovering guarded secrets.

The realization of another unforeseen danger caused Natalie to break out in tiny beads of perspiration. She ran her hand across her forehead. She thought about the last 24 hours, ghosts chasing Timothy, Devon with a mysterious wad of cash, and now syringes in James's room. She sighed heavily and felt pressure creeping up her neck and shoulders as she slumped to the floor.

She grabbed her face in her hands and screamed as loud as her voice would carry.

"What the hell is going on around here?!"

✝

CHAPTER 25

Natalie started up the stairs to Timothy's room. As she ascended the stairs, she could see that the door was open, but Timothy was not in his bed. She stopped at the door.

"Timothy?" Natalie peered in the room. Timothy was sleeping soundly rolled up in a wad of sheets on Anna's bed. Natalie walked over to the bed and rubbed his head.

"Timothy, honey, wake up. It's time to get up." He rolled over with a big stretch. His eyes slowly opened.

"Hey, sleeping beauty. How long have you been sleeping in here?"

"Just two nights, Mama." He yawned and let out a sigh of irritation for being asked questions he didn't want to answer.

"Why won't you sleep in your room?"

"I don't want to sleep in there ever again." His eyes squinted tightly shut as if to hide from another vision of Caroline. Natalie looked at Timothy with concern.

"Tell me what happened." Natalie wanted to know more, and had no intention of leaving until she found out.

"I saw Caroline Bradford in my room. I'm not sleeping in there anymore! I can't! I just can't!"

Timothy's eyes filled with tears. He rolled out of the bed and sat on the side, shaking his head. Natalie sat down beside him and put her arm around him.

"It's okay. We'll move your things today. There's another bedroom at the end of the hall." Timothy became quiet and nodded with relief. He took a deep breath and wondered if his nightmares were really over.

Several hours passed as Natalie and Timothy moved his furniture and other belongings to the room at the end of the second floor. No one had occupied the room, and it was far away from the terror behind the corner bedroom door. He busied himself with hanging posters and setting up his stereo.

Devon was late arriving home and Natalie wondered what his next excuse would be. She sat on the top step of the staircase and dialed Moore Distribution. The receptionist answered the phone on the first ring.

"Moore Distribution, may I help you?"

"Yes, Ma'am. This is Natalie Bradford. Can you tell me if Devon Bradford is still there?"

"No, Ma'am. His shift was over at 6:30 a.m. In fact, I passed him on my way in this morning."

"Oh- Ok, thank you for your help." Natalie held the receiver in her hand staring into space. She slowly placed the receiver on the phone base. Devon was lying to her about everything, the money, his whereabouts, and his need for a wife. And what about his innocence? What if he had been lying about that? Natalie felt helpless.

She looked all around the mansion studying the grandiose size. The house seemed to swallow her. She thought about Devon and how he had promised her a happy family life for her and her children. He had totally shut her out of her own dreams. Her mood turned to dread as reality closed in. It was becoming more and more apparent that Devon Bradford wasn't who she thought he was. She felt trapped between admitting she was wrong and hoping he would change.

Natalie started down the stairs for the master suite, scared to sleep in a house that wasn't hers and never would be. The stairs creaked with each step she made. The great room was dimly lit from the soft glow of a tableside lamp. The room seemed full of eyes as she stepped down each stair. She flinched with apprehension as she stared into the stillness that ached to burst forth with the anguish of Liz Bradford.

"Anna, shut the door and lock it." Natalie walked fast as she entered the master suite. She was exhausted and needed sleep. She got on her knees and looked under the bed searching for the loaded shotgun that once belonged to her father. Devon did not know she had the gun, and she had decided it was best not to tell him. Another day had gone by without hearing from her husband.

Anna watched her mother with curiosity. She had noticed a change in her mother, a change she rarely saw. Her mother was scared. And since Timothy had seen ghosts, she wasn't about to sleep alone upstairs if she didn't have to. She slammed the door shut and turned the lock, locking the two of them in the room. A sense of dread had started to consume Anna, and she didn't want to face the truth that she knew was coming. She knew they needed to leave Lindenwood.

Natalie read a book by Louis Lamour while Anna settled herself next to her mother. Natalie's eyes began to grow heavy after several minutes of flipping pages. The soft light from her bedside lamp burned steady as she moved into a deep slumber. The book slipped from her hands onto the floor. Within minutes, Natalie was completely unaware of her surroundings. She never heard the doorknob twist as it gently opened and rested against the doorstop.

The voiceless spirit of Liz Bradford swept across the bedroom floor. She stood as a silhouette above Natalie's head as she curiously looked at the body of another woman lying in her bed. Her face twisted in confusion as she glanced back and forth at Anna and Natalie. Then without warning, her face changed into a diabolical glare. She placed her hands in Natalie's hair and began to massage her scalp as she used to do with her customers in her own salon at Lindenwood.

Natalie began to stir, rolling from side to side as she felt the eerie presence of fingers sweeping through her hair. Suddenly she jerked awake as Liz Bradford tore at her hair. She reached back with her hands and felt her head. Hair rollers were wound tight all over her head, but she knew she hadn't rolled her hair before she lay down. She tried to lift herself from the bed but was met with a forceful push against her shoulders.

Natalie lay dead still, her breathing heavy and fast. She struggled against the tremendous pressure resting across her chest. She repeatedly tried to lift herself from the bed. Finally, with all her strength she pushed against an invisible force and jerked herself upright. She bolted from the bed and ran to the mirror.

She stood rigid, staring at the reflection in the glass. There were no hair rollers, but she knew she felt them. She whirled around inspecting the room. The bedroom door was standing wide open. Waves of terror covered Natalie's body as she realized she had not been alone inside the room. The only way to open the door would have been from the inside. Her body quivered as if she were standing in a bitter snowstorm. She surveyed the room again and walked over to Anna who was sleeping soundly.

A sudden revelation caused Natalie to gasp, her hand rushed over her mouth.

"Oh my God, Liz Bradford had been a hairdresser when she was alive!"

Chills covered her arms. Had the ghost of Liz Bradford come back to run her away from Lindenwood, the mansion she had claimed as hers only two years ago, or were these hallucinations caused by drugs? Was James Bradford drugging her and Timothy with PCP? Maybe he was putting it in her tea at night. She and Timothy were the only two people in the house that drank sweet tea. Everyone else drank Kool-aid. But could the drug have an effect diluted in liquid? She knew James was using drugs, but what and how much? And where was he getting it? Could that explain Devon's weird behavior and his fixation with money? How could she be asking herself these questions now? Why hadn't she questioned anything before?

Natalie shook her head. Her mind raced with desperation as she sought logical answers. It was clear she didn't know what she was dealing with at Lindenwood. Her face was pale. She sat down on the edge of the bed in silence, wringing her hands in an effort to warm them from the coldness of the room. She contemplated her next move. She had to leave Lindenwood for the night. She needed to see Margaret. No one else would believe what was happening to her and her children.

✝

CHAPTER 26

Natalie turned onto Elvis Presley Drive and followed the well-lit city street to Margaret's brick home. It was past 10:00 p.m. and her friend was already preparing for bed when she saw the headlights of the Oldsmobile through her bedroom window. Margaret pulled the curtain back and peered out the glass, her eyes squinted from the headlight's blinding glare.

Natalie turned the ignition off and turned around to look at Anna and Timothy slumped against the side of the car and sleeping in spite of the interruption. She opened the car door and grabbed the overnight bag she had hastily stuffed on her way out. Anna and Timothy stirred as she slammed the door shut and made her way around to the other side of the car.

"Come on, kids. We're at Margaret's. You can go back to sleep in there. Okay?" Natalie opened the car door and leaned forward to pick up Anna. Anna wrapped her arms around her mother's neck.

"What's going on?" Timothy mumbled half-asleep. His curly hair was tousled all over his head.

"Nothing. Now come on." Natalie motioned for Timothy to get out. She followed him up the steps to the front door where Margaret stood waiting under the glare of the front porch light.

"Natalie? What's going on?" She held the screen door open.

"Sh-h-h!" Natalie held her finger over her mouth. "I'll tell you in a minute. We need to stay tonight, Margaret."

Margaret nodded. "Of course. Put the kids in the guest room."

Natalie walked past Margaret and led Timothy down a hallway to a room with a queen size bed. She pulled the comforter back and laid Anna against the pillow while Timothy climbed on the opposite side. Natalie pulled the blankets close to Anna tucking her in and leaned over to pat Timothy on the back. She flicked the overhead light off and walked back to the kitchen where Margaret busied herself with brewing a pot of coffee.

"Hey, I'm making some coffee. I figured we'd probably need it. I've never known you to drag the kids out at this hour." Margaret's tone was inquisitive as she placed two coffee mugs on the counter.

"Yeah, you're right. I really need to talk to you. Something is going on at Lindenwood, and I'm getting scared." Natalie stood with her hands on the back of a kitchen chair as if she needed it for support.

Margaret sighed and motioned for Natalie to join her at the table. "Sit down, Nat. You look tired."

Natalie eased down in the wooden chair. Her neck and shoulders ached.

"I am tired, Marg. I am so tired, and you just don't know what has been going on. You may be right about Lindenwood."

Margaret's eyes were wide. "Haunted, you mean?"

"Maybe. You know I don't believe in that stuff, but my nerves are just about gone." Natalie's eyes began to moisten and her voice began to shake.

"Hey, it's okay." Margaret reached for Natalie's hand.

"Well-I guess it started with Devon. He's been acting really weird lately. Almost like he's another person. And he never comes home when he says he's going to. I don't know what to make of it. He won't help me financially. I might as well be on my own. Nothing has turned out the way I thought it would." Natalie shook her head in disgust.

"I'm sorry, Natalie. But, honestly, I'm not surprised." Margaret leaned back in her chair and studied Natalie's trembling hands.

"Natalie, are you in danger?"

Natalie's eyes were anxious and her voice to the point of hysteria.

"I don't know. Strange things have been happening around the mansion. Timothy's been having nightmares. He says he saw the ghost of Caroline Bradford, Marg. And now, I've had my own nightmare. Tonight, I felt someone rolling my hair, for God's sakes. My bedroom door was locked when I went to sleep. And when I woke, the door was standing wide open. No one can open that door from the outside."

Margaret felt ripples of fear sweeping up her back. "I told you, Nat. I told you. That damn place is haunted. How could it not be? I don't care how much money Devon Bradford's got or how good-looking he is-I wouldn't stay in that house for one minute."

"But, how can someone dead hurt you? Really, Margaret, do you know how crazy that sounds?" Natalie chewed her fingernail.

Margaret nodded but didn't offer an explanation. "So, if you don't believe in ghosts, why did you come all the way to Tupelo to spend the night?"

Natalie looked at Margaret with agreeing eyes. "Because you do believe in it, and if anyone might have an answer, it would be you."

She leaned toward Margaret. "Listen to me. Tonight, while I was in the bed, I tried to get away from whatever or whoever had their fingers in my hair, and I couldn't. I couldn't get away. Something was forcing me against the bed. It was across my chest and felt like a fifty-ton weight pressing me into the mattress."

Margaret ran her hands over her face. "I've heard of that happening. It's called *The Old Hag Syndrome*. I've heard the ghost holds you down then lets you go right before you pass out."

"But, why would Liz Bradford want to hurt me? I didn't kill her."

Margaret shook her head. "I don't believe she wants to hurt you. You know she cursed Devon before she died. You said he's been acting like a different person. I bet he's becoming possessed by a dark spirit."

"A dark spirit?" Natalie's eyes were frightful.

"Yeah. Just listen to me for a minute." Margaret held her hand in the air as if she wanted to stop Natalie from protesting.

"Based on what I know, a person has to be susceptible to the misfortune that is being willed upon them. Devon already had a love of money and love of himself. In a lot of ways, *he* was a dark soul. He's an easy target for possession, and Liz Bradford would only want to see his dismay after what he did to her."

"This sounds like something out of a horror show."

Margaret shrugged. "Yep, it does. But, it's possible. And you're not safe there. You never have been."

"I'm beginning to believe you, about my safety anyway."

"So, what's your next move? Are you going back to Lindenwood?"

"I have to, Marg. I think I'll talk to my brother and ask him to come bless the house. You know he's a minister."

Margaret stared at Natalie across the table. She wondered if Natalie realized what she was dealing with at the Lindenwood mansion. There was no way she could know. She was too naïve. If Devon Bradford had been successful in luring her into his lair, then she was surely not prepared for the truth she would be facing in just a few days.

CHAPTER 27

Natalie left early the next morning. By 6 a.m., she was back at Lindenwood in her own bed. She had to get home before Devon came home. She couldn't let him know that she was anywhere but Lindenwood. She lay against the pillow and closed her eyes drifting in and out of sleep. She was exhausted, almost lethargic from anxiety. The sun had just started to peek through the narrow windows of the master suite when the slamming of the front door echoed throughout the great room.

Devon Bradford walked through the bedroom door. His eyes were dark, void of emotion. His face was unshaven, his clothes wrinkled. He breathed deep as he stood over the king size bed watching the new Liz Bradford sleep in his house. Natalie stirred and opened one eye. As she caught a glimpse of Devon's zombie like stare, she jerked awake and sat up. A look of terror covered her face. She wasn't looking at the same man she married. He was someone else, sinister and foreboding. She swung her legs over the side and stood beside the bed.

"What are you doing, Devon?" She rushed past him to the bathroom.

"I'm wondering why you aren't awake. Aren't you going to work?" Devon's tone was louder than usual and demanding.

"Of course. It's only 6:00." Natalie started the water in the shower trying to busy herself away from Devon.

"Anna, get up and go to your room." Natalie called to Anna curled up in a ball on the bed. She slowly rolled off the side and walked out of the room.

Devon leaned against the bathroom door while Natalie got in the shower.

"You're not going to ask where I've been?" He tested her. She continued to wash her hair under the spray of water.

"Why should I? You made it clear a couple of days ago that it wasn't any of my damn business. I figure you can sit here and ponder the same question when you come home someday and I'm not here." Natalie wasn't going to be pushed around. She was tired, irritated, and hurt by Devon, but she would burn in hell before she gave him the satisfaction of knowing he could intimidate her.

Devon's blood ran cold. His eyes filled with rage. As Natalie opened the shower door and stepped out, Devon reached forward, grabbing her by the throat. His hands squeezed tight, pushing her back against the wall. She tried to cough as his fingers squeezed the breath from her. She stared at him with a look of horror, forcefully raising her knee to strike his groin. He slowly loosened his grip. Natalie spat and gasped for air.

"Don't ever threaten me, Natalie." Devon's voice was not his own but rather deep and loud opposite from his usual whisper.

Tears began to pour over Natalie's cheeks. "Why did you do that? Who are you? What's going on?" Natalie screamed from the pit of her soul. She cowered in the corner of the shower afraid Devon might choke her again.

"Talk to me, damn it! If you won't talk to me, please talk to our preacher. We've only been married for two months. I just can't- Devon, I can't stay here anymore!" Natalie felt defeated. As she stared in the face of an accused murderer, she began to see the man that Liz Bradford had been married to.

No." Devon whispered. He leered at Natalie as he stood over her. "You will not leave." Devon came at Natalie shouting in her face. "I said no!" Devon turned to leave, then stopped and pointed his finger at her. The sound that came from his lips sounded like a demon from hell. "Don't try to leave."

His eyes roamed over Natalie with disgust. "And change your damn hair. You look like that bitch buried across the highway."

Natalie sat in a daze, her mouth open in shock. She felt a chill sweep over her at the realization of Devon's words. The store clerk had told her that she favored Devon's deceased wife. Liz Bradford was dead, and possibly at the hands of her own husband and the man she had just married. Natalie chewed her fingernail and eased up the side of the wall. Her throat and neck were bruised, and the imprint of his hands still lingered on her skin. Natalie began to question her judgment. Nothing in the house had been moved since Liz died. All the décor was the same. She was simply a guest in someone else's home, someone dead.

Natalie didn't feel welcome at Lindenwood any longer, not by Devon or the ghost of Liz Bradford. She had stumbled into a nest of treachery and had been brainwashed by Devon Bradford. Was he even who he said he was? She had married a man full of secrets. Secrets she no longer wanted to know about. She knew she had to tread carefully until she could escape his hold. She had to watch what she said and whom she said it to. Devon couldn't know that she was getting suspicious.

Natalie clutched a bath towel as she sat down on the commode lid with her head in her hands and sobbed. The rush of reality was too much for her. Why had she fallen into a madhouse filled with ghosts and a man she had once believed was innocent? It would only be a matter of days before Natalie's tormented world would put her in the face of pure evil.

CHAPTER 28

The last four nights had not been restful for Natalie. Every morning she woke with the bedroom door standing open even though she had begun locking it from the inside. Her stomach churned and ached from the tension she was under. She didn't want to give up on her marriage. She was overwhelmed with grief. Another divorce was imminent. Her inner voice would not be silent now as she must accept the reality of her own failure to notice the signs that foretold her present circumstances.

Upstairs, Audrey and Susan whispered behind Susan's bedroom door.

"My curling iron is missing and so is my hairbrush." Susan said with aggravation.

"Well, my favorite bracelet is gone. Audrey included. I didn't take your stuff. Anna must be coming in here. Let's go look in her room."

The two girls briskly walked down the hall ready to confront Anna. She was just getting awake when she saw Audrey and Susan standing in her doorway.

"Anna, Audrey and I want our stuff back that you took." Susan wasted no time with her accusations.

Anna rubbed her eyes and propped up on her elbows with a look of confusion. "I haven't taken any of your stuff."

Audrey began to get loud as she supported her sister's accusations. "Then who did? You took my favorite bracelet, didn't you?"

Anna became angered and jumped out of bed. She yelled back. "I don't have your stupid bracelet, but my doll's rollers are missing! Maybe you took those!"

Hey, what's all the screaming about? Natalie shouted from the bottom of the stairs. You girls come down here, right now."

Audrey and Susan marched down the stairs with an air of defiance while Anna followed chewing her thumbnail.

"What's going on?" Natalie demanded an answer. All the shouting had also awakened Timothy who peered over the balcony.

"My curling iron and brush are gone and Audrey's favorite bracelet is missing."

"Have you looked for it?"

"Yes, but Anna is coming in our rooms."

Anna interrupted, shouting. "I am not!"

"Anna, hush. You'll get your turn. Why do you think Anna took it?"

"I don't know." Susan dropped her eyes and stared at the floor.

"You don't know. That's not a very good reason to blame her for it."

"Anna, have you been in their rooms? Tell the truth." Natalie's tone was firm, and her eyes were fixed on her daughter.

"Only when they knew I was there. My doll's rollers are gone, but I didn't blame them for it." Anna began to sob.

"Okay, girls. We'll all look for your things after school. No more fighting, and I mean it."

Timothy watched above them. He waited for Anna to come back upstairs. As she turned the corner, he motioned for her to come to his room.

"I know who's doing it, but no one will believe me."

"Why not?" Anna looked curiously at Timothy.

"They just won't."

"Who took my doll's rollers?"

"Caroline Bradford ." Timothy pointed to the window where the two graves of Liz and Caroline Bradford were visible.

"Don't be silly. They're not even alive."

"Well, no, not exactly, but they're definitely here. I promise you that. They are here."

✝

CHAPTER 29

It was past suppertime at Lindenwood. Natalie finished cleaning the dishes in the kitchen and began to wipe the bar area clean. Anna and Audrey sat at the dining room table studying schoolwork. Timothy's door was closed, but the music that crept under his door was loud enough to annoy Anna. She stared across the open area of the top floor to the door at the end of the long hall. The television played downstairs in the great room where a friend of James's sat on the black, leather sofa waiting while James showered.

Natalie had instructed Anna and Timothy to watch James, especially at supper. Natalie and Timothy drank their usual two glasses of tea. Anna and the rest of the Bradford children drank cherry kool-aid. Anna was in the kitchen when James had poured his glass, but she didn't notice him putting anything in her mother's or brother's glass. If James were drugging them, he would have to be doing it while no one was around, possibly after Natalie had left the kitchen.

Natalie flipped the light off and started for the stairs when Timothy opened his bedroom door. He stood in the doorway, his face void of color. Tears washed over his cheeks. Natalie stopped and stared at Timothy who stood still, flooded by the loud music coming from the room.

"Timothy? What's wrong with you, son?" Natalie's throat became tight, and her eyes began to moisten. She was scared.

Timothy was quiet, shaking his head.

"Come here, son." Natalie turned the corner of the staircase. Timothy began to take baby steps toward her.

"Timothy?" Natalie ran to him, her arms outstretched. She held him tight, rubbing his hair. "What's wrong with you?" Her voice was despondent.

Timothy jerked violently as he sobbed in his mother's arms. "Mama-

"What is it, Timothy? What?"

"I saw Papaw."

Natalie's skin tingled, and goose bumps covered her body. Her heart pounded as a wave of terror swept over her.

"What do you mean, you saw Papaw?"

"He-

Natalie sat back. She held Timothy's hands.

Timothy shook his head in amazement. "He was standing at the end of my bed, Mama. I swear I saw him. He even spoke to me!"

Natalie's mouth fell open. She waited for Timothy to say more.

"I asked him when I was gonna get to be with him in heaven."

"Timothy, you must've been dreaming. It's just a bad dream." Natalie tried to calm her son, but Timothy continued to shake his head.

"No, Mama! No! Papaw said I would be joining him 'very soon' in heaven!"

"Dear God!" Natalie pulled Timothy close. Tears silently poured down her cheeks. Her body trembled at the thought of what her son had just seen. What could he be going through? She had to get help or get him out of Lindenwood. She didn't believe in ghosts, but she remembered from her earlier Bible teachings that the devil could take on many disguises. That must be the answer to what was happening. Pure evil.

Anna and Audrey got up from the table. James's friend was sitting downstairs and had also been watching from the bottom floor when a terrifying creak came from the front door. As the guest watched in horror, the knob twisted and turned, and the door opened more than a foot wide.

"Oh, hell!" James's friend jumped to his feet.

All eyes were wide and fixed on the door waiting to see someone appear, but no one did. James's friend grabbed his keys from the sofa and ran out the door. As the door slammed behind him, the electricity flickered off and then on. Just as the lights flashed on, Audrey beheld the deceased soul of her sister, Caroline Bradford standing in the doorway of her bedroom at the corner of the second floor. Audrey's screams escaped from the depths of her soul with an undeniable force that expressed the fear and horror of what she saw. As her screams echoed throughout the mansion, the bedroom door slammed shut.

Natalie and the kids shook violently with fear. She struggled to gain control and calm the children as she felt herself crumbling beneath a gripping force of terror. Huddled together at the top of the stairs, Natalie held the children close. Audrey wept as she pointed to the corner of the staircase.

"My sister. I just saw my sister. She's in the b-bedroom". Audrey's speech was slurred.

"Just stay calm and stay right here. I'll go look." Natalie managed to get the children to loosen their grip as she slowly made her way around the second floor.

Natalie Bradford was scared now. A million thoughts raced through her mind. She couldn't believe this was happening. It deficd everything she had ever believed in. She walked to the closed bedroom door and reached for the doorknob. She twisted the knob, but it was locked. Someone had locked the door from the inside! And this was exactly the same thing that had been happening in her bedroom. There was no doubt in her mind. Lindenwood needed to be prayed over. It was now out of her hands.

✝

CHAPTER 30

Matthew Cooper drove his dark blue 1975 Crown Victoria up the long drive to Lindenwood. Sarah Cooper sat in the back seat giving him directions on where to park while his wife Barbara was quiet, waiting to intervene if a referee was needed. He turned the ignition off and got out of the car. He stretched his arms over his head and surveyed the property. He noticed the gravesites overlooking Lindenwood from across the highway. His facial expression showed his curiosity, and he wondered about the two buried women's souls.

Having served as a sergeant in World War II, Matthew Cooper knew what discipline and honor meant. He was a stern man, rigid in his beliefs and opinions, but also easily moved to tears. He didn't mind telling anyone what the Good Book had to say about how a person should live their life or how they should seek salvation through Jesus Christ. He believed in nothing other than The Word, and his convictions spoke strongly each time he took the pulpit.

Sarah and Barbara stood just inside the great room door talking to Natalie when Matthew walked in. He looked up the stairs to the second floor. He noticed the darkness of the mansion and took a deep breath. Peculiar smells in the air puzzled him. His stomach churned.

Natalie turned to greet her brother. He towered over her, standing almost 6 feet tall.

"Hey, Matthew. Come in. Would you like a glass of tea?"

"No- No, I don't think so." Matthew cleared his voice and shoved his hands in his pockets.

"I think we better go ahead and have prayer. We can't stay."

"What? You just got here." Natalie was shocked.

"Well, we've got church this evening."

Natalie looked at him with doubt. Church services were five hours away. It was just past lunch on an ordinary Sunday afternoon. The sun shined brightly through the open front door. A breeze caught the door causing it to swing back and forth.

Matthew turned and looked at the door. He reached for Natalie's hand. "Let us pray."

Sarah and Barbara joined hands while Audrey and Anna stood nearby with their heads bowed. Matthew's voice was earnest and sincere as he prayed.

"Dear Lord Jesus, bless the home of Devon and Natalie Bradford. Bless it with your almighty grace and holiness. Fill every room of this place with only your presence. Make Lindenwood a home of your will and anchor your spirit to reside in this place and in the hearts of all who live here. Cast out the wicked and forbid them from entry into this home. In your heavenly name, we pray. Amen."

Matthew opened his eyes. A gush of cold air swept past his face. A shooting pain ripped through his stomach, and he felt as if he were going to vomit. He held his Bible close to his side and motioned for Barbara and Sarah to follow him.

"Natalie, we'll see you soon."

"Well, I'm sorry to see you leave. I'd like to cook dinner for everyone." Natalie rushed to hug him.

"Oh, No. No." Matthew shook his head, and began to walk outside.

Sarah and Barbara looked puzzled, and followed Matthew out the door. They slammed the car doors shut and waved to Natalie as Matthew backed down the drive. Natalie looked perplexed as she waved back. Anna stood watching with her hands on her hips.

"Why did they leave so soon, Mama?" Anna had a feeling that her uncle had gotten spooked. He must have seen Caroline on the staircase, but was afraid to tell anybody.

"I don't know." Natalie mumbled.

As Sarah Cooper adjusted her dress, she wondered why Matthew left with such haste. She thought his behavior was bizarre. "Matthew, why did you rush us out of the house?"

Matthew twisted in his seat. He looked over his shoulder toward Sarah and then turned his eyes back to the road. He shrugged his shoulders.

She continued to press him. "Why, Matthew?"

Matthew tightened his grip on the steering wheel. "I didn't feel welcome there."

"Why in the world would you say that? Natalie asked you to come." Sarah asked in disbelief.

Matthew shook his head. "It wasn't Natalie. I don't know what it was to be honest, but *something* just came over me, and I felt a powerful urge to leave."

✝

CHAPTER 31

Anna pushed against the back door.

"Hurry up, Anna. I've got to pee." Audrey ordered.

Both of the girls had just gotten off the school bus. No one was home yet. Audrey helped Anna push the door open. The door swung open and Audrey ran for the small powder room in the den. Anna slammed the door shut behind them. She walked through the den into the great room. The house was filled with a musky odor that hung heavy near the entrance to the master suite.

"Shoo, something stinks."

Anna proceeded near her mother's bedroom. She rubbed her nose. Suddenly she froze just outside her mother's doorway. She peered around the door into the room. Someone was wrapped in a bed sheet lying in her mother's bed. She saw hair peeking from beneath the sheets at the front of the bed, but there was no movement. Anna took small breaths afraid to make any noise. She felt certain that the person in the bed was not her mother, but she had to be sure.

"Mama?" Anna tiptoed just inside the door. The body never moved. Anna's heart began to pound. She backed out of the doorway just as Audrey entered the room. Anna put her finger over her mouth and motioned for Audrey to come see, but when she turned back around she noticed the front door standing open.

"We've gotta get out of here. Someone's in Mama's bed." She whispered in a panic.

Not doubting Anna, Audrey ran for the door and bolted down the driveway with Anna close behind screaming. "Go across the highway! We'll call Mama from the store!"

Within seconds the girls were inside the old country store filled with empty cases of Coca-Cola bottles in each corner. The elderly man dressed in his customary pair of overalls sat behind the counter shucking corn.

"Noon, girls."

"Can I use the phone to call my mama?" Anna panted, out of breath.

"Okay, go ahead." He pointed to the phone hanging on the wall.

Anna dialed her mother's work. Her face was flushed and her mouth dry. She danced on her toes, impatiently waiting for her mother to answer the phone.

"County Medical Clinic, Nurse Bradford speaking."

"Mama, someone's in our house!" Anna was frantic.

"What?"

"I saw them. In your bed, rolled up in a sheet, and the front door is open."

"Anna, where are you?"

"Across the street, at the store."

"Okay, stay out of the house until I get home." Natalie hung up the phone. She took a deep breath and wondered if Anna's claim was real. Was it a child's overactive imagination or was someone unknown in her house? She couldn't be sure, especially with everything going on at Lindenwood. She laid her pen down and grabbed her sweater as she raced out the door.

Natalie arrived at Lindenwood thirty minutes later. She saw the front door standing open. Anna and Audrey were sitting on the front porch waiting for her. Natalie flung the car door open and walked briskly across the lawn.

"Are you okay?" Natalie opened her arms to hug Anna.

"Uh-huh." Anna followed her mother in the house.

Natalie eased the door open. She carefully entered the giant great room, making her way to the master suite. Natalie peeked around the door. The bed linens were lying in disarray on the floor at the foot of her bed. Natalie noticed her pillow on the floor. She didn't remember knocking it off the night before.

Natalie turned and left the room. She walked back onto the porch where Audrey was still playing jacks.

"Audrey, did you go in the house with Anna when you got home from school?"

"Yes, Ma'am." Audrey stopped her ball from bouncing and turned looking up at Natalie.

"What did you see in my bedroom?"

"I saw a dead woman. She was lying on the same side of the bed where you sleep."

"A dead woman?" The familiar feeling of fear swept over the length of her body paralyzing her for the moment.

Audrey spoke with assuredness. "Yes, Ma'am. A ghost. But I think it was just my mama." She turned back around and began playing with her jacks.

Natalie felt the hair rising on the back of her neck.

"Anna, go upstairs and pack an overnight bag. We're going to Grandma's."

✝

CHAPTER 32

Natalie rushed in the house and skipped a step as she climbed the stairs. She grabbed a few of Timothy's clothes before running downstairs to gather her own. As much as she regretted it, she would have to leave Audrey in her two older sister's care until Devon came home. And she knew she must hurry before Devon arrived and caught her leaving.

Natalie shoved her things in the Oldsmobile. "Anna, let's go." She slammed the door shut.

Audrey watched from the upstairs balcony as Natalie accelerated down the drive. She felt a familiar feeling of loneliness, and silently wished her new mother would come back.

Sarah Cooper worked diligently pruning the red rose bushes along her front porch flowerbeds. Her wide brimmed blue hat shielded her face as the sun began to go down. She had been working in her yard for most of the afternoon when Natalie pulled into the steep driveway.

Anna jumped out of the car and rushed over to her Grandmother. Timothy took his time unloading the trumpet he carried from band practice.

"Natalie, are y'all okay?" Sarah looked surprised as she laid the pruning shears down on the porch step.

"Mother, something strange is going on at Lindenwood. The kids don't want to sleep in their rooms, and I'm having horrible nightmares."

"Let's go inside and sit down. Where is Devon?" Sarah rubbed the back of Anna's hair and reached for her hand before climbing the porch steps.

"That's a good question. I don't know. He has totally shut me out in the last few weeks, and I don't know what to make of all this. He acts like a different person."

Sarah stared at the ground. She knew her daughter had gotten involved with Devon Bradford far too soon, but she had never been able to discourage Natalie's strong will without causing tension between them. She decided long ago that Natalie couldn't be persuaded to do anything opposite of what she wanted to do. Even though she seldom heeded Sarah's advice, her mother refused to stop giving it.

Natalie started for the door. Sarah followed her pulling off her garden gloves. The house was cool and peaceful. The aroma of freshly baked cornbread filled the small cottage. Natalie felt a sense of relief as she flopped down on the sofa. Sarah sat down in her cherished red rocker that she had owned since becoming a widow in 1968.

"Natalie, I have a bad feeling about that man. I'm afraid he needed you to get his kids out of foster care so he would look good in the eyes of the jury. Do you really believe he didn't kill that woman?"

"Well, he swore to me that he was innocent. You know I had to believe him in order to marry him." Natalie looked worried.

"But, now you're not so sure?"

"I don't know. I want to tell you something, but I know you'll just worry."

"Tell me anyway. I worry when I have nothing to worry about."

Natalie took a deep breath. "Devon is acting really strange. He's mean, and he's been lying to me about the places he goes. He is not the same person whom I knew just a few months ago. And, I'm afraid to ask any questions. He always has lots of cash, but he won't give me any at all."

Sarah listened intently, rocking back and forth in her chair. Her eyes were focused on Natalie.

"But, something else scares me more than that. My friend, Margaret told me something that she had heard about Devon's wife. She said Liz Bradford cursed Devon before she died. Margaret thinks Devon is becoming possessed, and I swear, I don't know what to think. Devon's face has even changed. He looks like the devil."

Sarah stopped rocking and leaned forward. She reached for her Bible, a King James edition. Its cover was faded and worn from years of use. Her voice was commanding. "Natalie, for once in your life, you need to listen to me." She flipped through the pages as if her eyes were closed. She knew the Scriptures and could recall many from memorization. Her fingers stopped in the book of John 8:44. She read aloud.

"The Lord said. 'Ye are of your father the devil, and the lusts of your father ye will do. He was a murderer from the beginning, and abode not in the truth, because there is no truth in him. When he speaketh a lie, he speaketh of his own: for he is a liar, and the father of it.'"

Natalie rubbed her head. The past two weeks of torment burst forth as tears dropped over her eyelids in a waterfall of anguish. "I feel so defeated. I have failed again, and I'm scared. What can I do?"

Sarah was angry. She wanted to blame someone else for her daughter's poor judgment. She shook her head and looked at Natalie with concern. "You know you can come here. You don't have to stay at Lindenwood. Devon Bradford is a clever man, and he fooled you, but you can overcome this."

"I'm scared, Mother. I think he might try to kill me."

"That's all the more reason to leave, Natalie. Listen to yourself. What did you just say?" Sarah's tone was laced with desperation. Natalie must come to her senses, and Sarah knew she had to intervene and risk alienating her daughter.

Sarah flipped through her Bible again. She grabbed a blank sheet of paper from her chair side table and began to copy a verse from 1 Peter 5:8 and 1 Peter 5:10. She handed the paper to Natalie. "Here. I want you to put this in a place where you can see it at all times. This is the Lord's promise. Believe it."

Natalie studied the scripture. She read aloud. "Be sober, be vigilant; because your adversary the devil, as a roaring lion, walketh about, seeking whom he may devour. But the God of all grace, who hath called us unto his eternal glory by Christ Jesus, after that ye have suffered awhile, will make you perfect, stable, and strong."

"Get out now, Natalie before it's too late. Give up this battle."

Natalie nodded then looked at her mother with confusion. "Mom, Devon is even talking crazy. He says that I remind him of his dead wife."

Sarah sat forward in her chair. Her body went rigid and cold as an uncanny knowing swept over her. She knew what was coming. She sensed it. Devon Bradford had gone mad, and Natalie must leave now or risk certain death.

Natalie wrung her hands as she contemplated her next move. She knew that she was experiencing a darker side of Devon Bradford, and it would only mean that time was ticking away until he made her his next victim. It was a truth she had desperately been trying to avoid in her ongoing denial.

"Natalie, I want you to get out of there now. Come stay with me as long as you need. Matthew will help get your things later." Sarah's tone was commanding.

Natalie looked at Sarah and realized her mother's fear for her safety. "Mom, give me a few more days." Even as she spoke, she was overcome with a dreadful premonition that would lead her straight into a hellish nightmare.

CHAPTER 33

The following afternoon Natalie returned to Lindenwood. Devon was waiting for her when she walked through the door. He sat on the edge of the sofa puffing on a cigarette. Only the setting sun gave the dark room any light. His shirt was unbuttoned exposing his chest, and his shoes were muddy. His hair was uncombed, and his face looked to have a full two days of beard growth. Lines in his face traced across his forehead as he was consumed in thought until Natalie appeared in the doorway. The door squeaked as she pushed it open with her suitcase.

She stood still, not daring to enter. Devon cut his eyes slowly from the floor to meet hers. A chilling evil emitted beneath his lids as he stared at her in a trance-like state.

"Hello, Devon." Natalie's voice shook. Anna and Timothy pushed past her and went up the stairs to their rooms. Natalie had made up her mind. She wouldn't dare let Devon know about her suspicions. She feared letting him know she was on to him. Devon continued to stare at her in silent disapproval. Finally, she eased past him and walked out of the room.

It was 10:30 p.m. Natalie locked the bedroom door. She walked back to the bed and flopped down resting her head on the pillow. She was relieved that Devon was gone to work and she wouldn't have to tiptoe around him for a few hours. He hadn't spoken to her much during the evening, ignoring her out of anger that she had gone to her mother's without telling him. Anna slept soundly beside her as she switched off the bedside lamp.

Suddenly, Natalie leaped from the bed. She heard a doorknob twisting in the den. The sound quickly escalated to a terrifying force of splitting wood as someone attempted to pry the locks off the den's back door. Natalie was terrified. The telephone was sitting on the end table outside her bedroom door. If she opened the door, the intruder might hear her. She stood frozen in the dark. Her breathing was shallow and beads of sweat moistened the bridge of her nose.

She knelt down on the floor and swept her hands under the bed searching for the shotgun she had hidden. She grabbed the gun with one hand and quietly crawled to the door. She listened too afraid to breathe. She clutched the gun close to her chest and watched the bottom of the door. She heard the shuffling of feet across the carpet. The intruder was now in the house and moving rapidly toward her room. The beam of a flashlight shone under her door. Natalie's breaths became quick as she steadied the shotgun. The doorknob twisted and stopped. Just as quickly as the footsteps were heard, they vanished.

Natalie let out a sigh of relief and leaned against the wall. She sat guarding the door for two hours until exhaustion took control of her body. She struggled to keep her eyes open. She fought against her need for sleep until her body ached. Soon she was overwhelmed and fell into a deep slumber. She woke hours later as the sun's warm rays washed over her face. Her body was stiff from lying slumped sideways against the door. The gun still rested in her arms, and the locked bedroom door that she had been guarding was standing wide open.

✝

CHAPTER 34

Natalie heard Audrey, Rebecca, and Susan upstairs in the kitchen. She wiped her eyes and stood up from the floor. Anna was still sleeping. She left the room headed for the den. As she walked through the door, she gasped when she saw the backdoor standing partially open with splinters of wood scattered across the floor.

Natalie turned and ran for the phone. She picked up the receiver to dial the sheriff's department when Devon walked through the door.

"Natalie, what happened to the backdoor?" Devon looked surprised.

Natalie laid the receiver down. "Someone tried to break in here last night. They even came to our bedroom door with a flashlight and I-

Natalie began to sob.

Devon went to put his arms around her. "Sh-h-h. It's okay now."

"No, it's not. I'm scared to stay here anymore. Strange things keep happening to me. I think I'm losing my mind sometimes, and you're never here." Tears poured from her eyes, her body shook as she buried her face in Devon's chest.

Devon gently stroked her hair. She rested her head on his shoulder. She thought to herself if only Devon would change, her life would be better.

"I'll take a day off tomorrow. I'm sorry you've been going through all of this by yourself."

Natalie wiped her face and looked up at Devon. He held her face in his hands. "Would you? Oh, Devon, we need to talk so bad. I need to tell you about James."

Devon pushed Natalie away from him. "What do you mean?" His voice turned harsh and suspicious.

Natalie stuttered. "I-

"I think he's using drugs, Devon." Natalie regretted her words as fast as she had spoken them.

"Natalie, you shouldn't concern yourself with my children. I'll deal with them, and I'll stop at nothing to protect them." His tone was a warning to her. She stood in disbelief as she watched him walk away from her. His demeanor changed as quickly as a faucet being turned off. How could he have just been holding her?

"I'm going to see if I can fix this door." Devon continued to ignore her.

"Don't you think we need to report this to the police?"

"Yeah, I'll call the sheriff's office in a minute."
He had no sense of urgency.

Natalie let out a sigh of disgust and shook her
head. She realized things would probably never change
and wondered how her life had taken such a drastic turn
in a short time. Everything seemed unpredictable.
Trouble and bizarre events she couldn't explain appeared
at every turn. She had never felt this insecure and scared
in all her life.

She watched Devon turn the corner. She ran and
grabbed the phone and hid behind the bedroom door.
Her hands trembled as she dialed Sarah Cooper's
number.

"Hello?"

"Mother?" Natalie's tone was frantic as she
whispered in the receiver.

"What's the matter?" Sarah immediately
recognized her daughter's voice.

"Listen. I have to whisper. I don't want Devon to
hear me."

"I'm leaving tomorrow. I'm going to pack as
much of our things as I can, and I'm leaving. I need to
stay with you for a few weeks." Natalie peeked again
through the crack in the door as she watched for Devon.

"Are you okay? Sarah began to pace the floor.

"Yeah, I'm okay, but I'm afraid I won't be if I
don't leave here." Natalie paused for a moment. She
cupped her hand around the phone and whispered even
lower.

"I think Devon lied about his wife's death."

Sarah became distraught as she ordered Natalie out of the house. "Natalie, don't you stay there another minute. Do you hear me? Come on now."

"No, Mother. I'll talk more about this tomorrow. I'll see you late tomorrow night. Now don't worry. I'll be fine."

Sarah yelled in the receiver. "Natalie, don't hang up this phone. You better not stay there. Do you hear me?" As the phone went silent on Natalie's end, Sarah Cooper began to cry.

She was in deep distress as she paced the kitchen floor. Her mind raced with worry not knowing what she should do. She decided if Natalie wasn't going to listen to her, then she would have to call her son, Matthew. He would have to go get her. Sarah picked up the phone and dialed Matthew.

Natalie eased from behind the bedroom door. She chewed her fingernail contemplating her next move. She had no idea that her every move was being watched and scrutinized. While she was confiding in her mother, Devon Bradford had managed to hide himself outside the door. And he had listened to every word she had spoken, his eyes fixed in a diabolical stare.

CHAPTER 35

Richard Oliver sat at his desk chewing on the end of a cigar. Piles of paperwork surrounded the attorney, cases he was working on for the D.A.'s office. He had already been at work for 3 hours, and it was only past 9 a.m.

Natalie sat on the floor outside her bedroom door. She held a telephone book in one hand and the receiver in the other. She dialed the county attorney's office in Tupelo after she was told by the D.A.'s office that Richard Oliver had been in charge of collecting the facts for the Bradford case.

Oliver picked up the phone without looking in its direction. "Oliver."

"Is this the county prosecutor's office?" Natalie didn't understand Oliver's quick, clipped speech.

"Yes, it is. This is Richard Oliver."

"Hi, Mr. Oliver. This is Natalie Houston. I'm calling you regarding a case you worked on last year. I'm hoping you can tell me something about the evidence."

"Who was it?"

"His name was Devon Bradford. Do you remember that case?"

Oliver immediately recognized the name. He sat up in his chair and rubbed his face as he recalled the proceedings. "Who are you?"

"I am his wife. He and I married a couple of months ago. He told me he was innocent, but since I've been with him, I've learned that he's a different man."

Oliver wasn't sure he wanted to continue the conversation. "What do you want to know? I don't know if I can help you."

"I was wondering if you could tell me about the first trial?" Natalie already knew the verdict but wanted to see what the prosecutor would tell her.

Oliver hesitated and took a deep breath. "Yeah, the best I can remember, he was convicted of manslaughter and sentenced to twelve years. But, some of those years were suspended."

"Manslaughter? Why not murder?"

"We tried him for murder, and the D.A.'s office sought life in prison, but the evidence wasn't strong enough to get a murder conviction."

"Do you know why he went to trial again?" Natalie pressed the prosecutor for more information. She wanted to keep him on the phone as long as he was willing.

"The State Supreme Court overturned the conviction. I think it was because of the police department's poor handling of the evidence. That happens."

"So, he could be guilty, and go free?" Natalie was appalled.

Oliver nodded his head toward the phone. "Absolutely."

"Did you know Devon Bradford?" Natalie hoped he would tell her something new.

"No, I didn't know him. Tell me again, why are you asking about this?" Oliver sounded suspicious.

"I'm in a dangerous situation, Mr. Oliver. I don't know who I married."

Oliver grunted. "Sounds like you should consider finding another place to live." Oliver cared about people, but he had to be careful about how he gave advice.

Natalie heard a door open in the den. She hastily ended the conversation. "Yes, sir. Thank you for your help."

She jerked around to see who had entered the room, but no one was seen. She hadn't been too smart by calling the attorney from Lindenwood, but it was too late.

James Bradford gently put the phone back on its hook, and closed the backdoor behind him. He walked straight to his car and headed for Devon Bradford's office.

CHAPTER 36

Natalie ran a brush through her wavy, soft hair. She examined herself in the mirror as she finished applying lipstick. Her eyes looked tired from the last several weeks of anxiety. In spite of the needed rest she had gotten at her mother's, she knew her sanity wouldn't stabilize until she was free from Lindenwood.

Natalie gathered her keys off the nightstand and headed for the door. She was working from 3 p.m. to 11 p.m. at the local hospital. Her plan was in place. She and the children were leaving as soon as she could get home. She stopped at the bottom of the stairs.

"Anna." Natalie called to her daughter. Anna was upstairs in her room dressing her three favorite Barbie dolls. She laid them on the bed and peeked out the door over the stair rail where Natalie waited below.

"Come down here." Natalie whispered urgently.

Anna hurriedly made her way down the stairs.

"While I am at work, I want you and your brother to pack all of your things that you can. You need to pack enough clothes for two weeks, Anna. Do you understand?"

Anna nodded.

"And take all of your toys that you will want."

"Why?" Anna stood still listening to her mother. She felt a sense of relief to be leaving Lindenwood. She wouldn't have to be scared anymore of the unseen eyes that followed her all throughout the house.

"Just do as I say, and don't tell anyone what you're doing, especially Devon." Natalie kissed Anna on the cheek.

"I'll see you after awhile." She walked out the front door and took a long look at the front of Lindenwood. Her eyes roamed over the stately columns lining the front porch. Her safety and sanity meant more to her now than a house that was never hers to begin with.

Eight hours later, Natalie Bradford walked out the swinging doors of the Emergency Room. She crossed the dimly lit parking lot to her car, careful to watch all around her. She let out a sigh as she slammed the car door shut. She ran her hands through her hair as she thought about not having to spend another night at Lindenwood. She knew she had to get out fast.

She pulled out of the parking lot and onto the dark highway toward Lindenwood. She lit a cigarette and puffed on it as she searched for music on the radio. Her eyes were heavy and she hoped the music would help her stay awake.

The city lights began to fade as Natalie made her way down the curvy, rural highway. It was past 11 p.m. and only two cars had passed her on the desolate road. The quietness scared her. The Oldsmobile rounded the last curve in the road about a mile from Lindenwood when a car with glaring headlights came at her head on. Natalie swerved to the other lane blowing her horn. The screeching of tires echoed in the darkness. She tried to catch her breath. She slowed to 40 miles per hour and looked in her rearview mirror.

The other car sat sideways in the road, smoke rolling from beneath the car. Swiftly, the smoke pillowed from the back tires screeching as the car sped fast toward her.

Natalie screamed, tears filling her eyes. She realized that whoever was driving the other car had meant to run her off the road. "Oh, God, help me!" Natalie screamed her prayers.

Natalie buried her foot into the accelerator. The unknown assailant made one last attempt to force Natalie Bradford into the huge trees alongside the road. The car hovered beside her. She breathed heavily as she glanced over in the darkness. She couldn't see the face of the driver. It was too dark. She thought she saw a black hood, and the shiny silver barrel of a gun being pointed directly at her.

Natalie slammed on the brakes. Her car slid on the pavement leaving skid marks, while the other vehicle drove ahead as if nothing had happened. Natalie sat in the darkness for a few seconds. She watched the tail lights of the car disappear before she decided to drive on. Her hands trembled as she tried to hold the steering wheel. She wiped her face and swallowed hard before driving toward the house. Her body shook with violence, her nose dripping with mucus and tears. Finally, she saw the lights of Lindenwood and raced up the drive.

✝

CHAPTER 37

Tears of horror and distress continued to stream down Natalie's face. She hastily put her keys in the lock and pushed the door open. The house was dark as usual. She made her way to the living room and up the stairs to check on the children. She first peeked in on Susan and Audrey before finding Anna and Timothy sleeping soundly in their beds. She made her way back downstairs and flicked off the outside lights on her way to the master suite.

Natalie immediately packed an overnight bag. She hurriedly stuffed clothes in the satchel and hid it under the bed. She closed the bedroom door and locked herself in while she changed out of her white nurse's uniform and into a pair of jeans and t-shirt. Devon would not be home until tomorrow morning, but she was too scared to waste any more time. As she gathered her jewelry and toiletry items, she thought she heard footsteps on the front porch.

Natalie held her breath. The sound was coming from the back of the house in the den. The rattling of the door being pried open woke Susan in her upstairs bedroom. She sat up in bed and listened to the sound of wood splitting. Downstairs, Natalie desperately tried to find her father's shotgun. She searched the floor and closet and found the gun hidden under the chaise lounge. She didn't remember putting it there.

Susan mustered up all the braveness she could and leaped from her bed. She ran down the stairs to Natalie's room. She pounded on the door.

"Let me in, Natalie. Please, hurry." She whispered loudly.

Natalie jerked the door open. Susan ran in and Natalie slammed the door shut, locking it. She ran to the far side of the bed and grabbed the shotgun with both hands. The gun was still loaded.

"Do you hear it? Someone's trying to kill us!" Susan gasped. Her heart was pounding, her speech slurred and broken in paranoia.

"Yes, I've been hearing it, but it's coming from all over the house. Come on, let's get upstairs, and you get on the phone."

"Whisper! They may already be in the house."

The rattling of glass came again, this time from downstairs in the den. Susan screamed and fell to the floor in terror. She crawled up the stairs to the phone hanging on the wall. Natalie followed skipping a step as she went. Susan grabbed the telephone cord and jerked the phone from the receiver. Her hands shook as she dialed the police.

Natalie huddled close to Susan, the shotgun against her chest. Suddenly a shadow appeared in the opening at the foot of the stairs. Natalie clutched the shotgun tighter as she placed her aim in the direction of the shadow.

Devon carried his pistol at his side as he rounded the corner of the stairs. He slowly entered the great room where Natalie and Susan stood waiting above.

"Devon!" Natalie shouted. Anna and Timothy woke at the sound of her voice and rushed to the bedroom doorway.

"You kids get back in your rooms now!" Natalie ordered.

Natalie fixed her eyes on Devon who started up the stairs toward them. "Devon, where did you get that gun?" Thoughts raced through her mind. He was once a convicted felon! At one time, it was against the law for him to own a gun and now he stood before her with a dead-on aim for her heart.

Susan backed up against the wall. "Daddy, what's wrong with you? What are you doing?" She yelled at her father as he walked in silence.

He never heard Susan's voice. He moved like a zombie, his purpose clear. A mist of evil flooded his glasslike eyes. He stopped halfway up the staircase and stared at the new Mrs. Bradford. He couldn't see Natalie Houston. She was no longer there. His ex-wife had come back from the grave, destined to leave him again, making a fool out of him.

Natalie pointed the shotgun at Devon's chest. "Devon, What are you doing? Have you gone crazy?" She realized that Devon had been the intruder all along. He had to be using drugs. He looked possessed with an evil no human had ever witnessed. Was this the image that Liz Bradford last saw while she was alive?

He froze. His eyes pierced her body, hypnotic. His lips barely moved as he spoke in a voice not his own.

"Tonight, I stood on a mountain. The dark of the night surrounded me. God stood to my right and Lucifer to my left. I was given a choice. When I chose Satan my heart turned to stone."

Natalie shook. Her eyes were full of terror. "Stop, Devon. Don't you come another inch, or I'll shoot. I swear I will!"

Devon laughed a boisterous heavy laugh. "You are so pathetic. You cannot leave me. Haven't you figured that out? You're the new Liz Bradford." Devon raised his gun. His finger rested against the trigger pull.

The room seemed to spin around Natalie. She knew she was going to die as Liz Bradford had if she didn't get out. She screamed and raised her foot as high as she could, kicking Devon in the chest. He slid down the stairs, and fell against the wall.

"Anna and Timothy, come on!" She screamed for her children as she held the shotgun at Devon's chest while her children ran down the stairs. Susan sat against the wall watching her father as he moaned. The last thing Devon Bradford heard was the Oldsmobile's screeching tires as she escaped.

✝

CHAPTER 38

Natalie listened as the phone rang repeatedly at Lindenwood. It had been three days since she and the children had left. She had only one reason to return to Lindenwood. She would be getting the rest of her clothes until her brother could help her move her things. Natalie was ashamed to admit that she had married someone she barely knew, but like other men in her life she hadn't been able to resist his charming ways.

Natalie hung up the phone after no one answered. She chewed her bottom lip. The sun was going down, and Devon should be on his way to work.

"If I sneak out there now, I can get our things without running into him." She spoke aloud.

She was still fearful of him and had to avoid seeing him at any cost. She grabbed her purse. The .38 caliber revolver her mother had loaned her was just inside the side pocket. She rushed out the door.

Natalie cautiously drove near the house. The lights were out in the mansion and there weren't any vehicles in the drive. Only the fluorescent lights from the old country store across the highway provided light as she turned onto the property. Natalie hurriedly walked to the front door. As she reached for the handle, the door suddenly opened. She clutched the pistol tightly in her hand as she stared at the door.

"Hello?" There was only silence.

Natalie pushed the door open with her foot and fumbled for the light switch in the great room. The house was untouched just as she left it. She shut the door behind her, locking the deadbolt. She ran up the stairs to the children's room.

Their bags were still sitting by their beds. She quickly grabbed the bags and ran down the stairs. She opened the front door and flung the bags on the porch before rushing back inside to the master suite where her own bags lay hidden under the bed. Natalie left the door ajar so as not to waste any more time.

She tugged on the small nylon bag shoved under the narrow hideaway. Suddenly, she heard the front door slam shut. She gasped looking for a place to hide. Then without warning, her bedroom door swung shut. Natalie ran for the door, grabbing the doorknob, but it was no use. She was met with a force she could not defeat.

Natalie screamed. She desperately jerked on the door trying to escape. She felt a chill and looked all about the room in horror. Natalie banged and jerked on the door.

Natalie began to cry great wails of pain. Devon Bradford had trapped her. She twisted and yanked the doorknob with all her might, kicking the door in an attempt to break it down. The lock on the door clicked and the doorknob turned. Natalie's breathing was heavy and labored as she watched the door slowly open a few inches. She grabbed the door and flung it open.

She was alone in the mansion. No one but the invisible force that had locked her in was present. She bolted for the front door, slamming it behind her. She flung her bags in the car. Her hands trembled as she started the car's engine and sped backwards down the drive not bothering to look back. As she wheeled the car around on the highway, she looked up the hill where the grave of Liz Bradford overlooked the grand mansion. An eerie mist stood suspended over her grave, and Natalie Bradford whispered a final goodbye as a sense of relief swept over her.

CHAPTER 39

Several weeks passed. Natalie Bradford wouldn't be spending the Thanksgiving or Christmas holidays with Devon Bradford. And she didn't want to waste time getting out of a marriage she had realized as a terrible mistake.

Natalie made an appointment to see an attorney. She thought about what she would carry with her from the marriage to Devon Bradford. Thoughts filled her mind as she reminisced about their courtship, the second trial, and his children that she had come to love. The youngest child, Audrey often called her "mama". She silently grieved for the little girl as she waited in the office lobby.

"Come in, Mrs. Bradford." The attorney was a short man with thick hair and dark skin.

"Hello." Natalie extended her hand.

"Mrs. Bradford, how will you be filing?"

"I want a no-fault divorce, please. I made a terrible mistake, and I need the quickest way out of this."

"I understand. Is there anything you will be dividing?"

"No, Sir. I wasn't there long. I'll just take my own furniture that I brought with me."

"Okay." The attorney scribbled on a notebook.

"But, sir, there is one thing I would like to have." Natalie paused and thought about the father of her children.

"What's that?" The attorney laid his pen down and sat back in his chair.

Natalie spoke with certainty. "I want my name back."

Later that afternoon, Natalie left the attorney's office and drove to the circuit clerk's office where Devon's trial had been held. She needed to see the court records from Devon's first trial. There were questions that she needed answered.

She walked in the courthouse and looked all around. The huge building smelled of old papers and mildew. She wandered in the back room and flipped through file after file until she finally located the Bradford case.

She opened the front cover of the file and noticed the court log. There in black ink was today's date staring her in the face. It read, February 6th, 1975 Devon Bradford was indicted for the murder of Liz Bradford. Cold chills swept over her. How could it be that she had filed for a divorce on the exact same day that he was indicted for her murder? Natalie's hand rested on her mouth in awe. She thought about their marriage date, and fell back against her chair, realizing she had married Devon on the same day as Liz Bradford's birthday. How could she have been so oblivious to everything that was transpiring before her eyes?

Natalie closed the file and rushed out of the courthouse. She drove steadfast to her mother's home where she found Sarah gardening in her front yard.

"Hey, Mom." Natalie slammed the car door shut.

"Natalie, you look like you have just seen a ghost. What's wrong?" Sarah studied her daughter's face.

"Mom, can we sit down?" Natalie started for the door.

"Sure, go on in." Sarah followed her up the porch steps and shut the screen door behind them locking it.

"Is everything ok?" Sarah sat down in her favorite rocker.

"Uh, yes, yes. Everything is ok now, but I have discovered something that I just don't know how to digest."

"What is going on?" Sarah's tone was apprehensive.

Natalie sighed and rubbed her forehead. "Mom, this is going to sound ridiculous, but I think that I have been a part of a prophecy of some sort. I just did some digging at the courthouse and found out that Devon was indicted for the murder of his wife on February 6, 1975."

Sarah looked confused. "Today is February 6th. What are you getting at?"

"Liz Bradford was trying to leave Devon. The only thing she wanted was a divorce. Mom, I just filed for a divorce today. It's now on record."

"That's incredible."

"Wait, it doesn't end there. I also found out that Liz Bradford's birthday was August 5th. That is our wedding anniversary."

Sarah cleared her throat and shifted in her chair. "Oh Lord, Natalie no wonder you had so much trouble."

"But don't you see? Devon kept telling me that I was the new Mrs. Bradford. It all makes sense now, but on the other hand it doesn't. Nothing makes logical sense. What do you think?"

"It makes perfect sense to me. Liz Bradford's spirit wasn't at rest. And, yes you were an instrument used to reveal the truth."

"Unbelievable!" Natalie leaned back against the sofa.

Sarah and Natalie sat in silence contemplating the last few months events when the telephone's ring jolted them back to reality.

"Don't get up, Mom. I'll get it." Natalie slowly stood up and started for the kitchen. She lifted the phone receiver from the wall.

"Hello?"

Hello, is this Natalie Bradford?" Natalie flinched upon hearing herself called "Bradford."

"Who is this?" The skin on her neck began to tingle.

"This is Suzanne, Devon's fiancé. I hope I didn't catch you at a bad time, but I was hoping you could help me." The woman's voice was pleasant and sincere, but Natalie was suspicious. She didn't answer the woman, intent on discouraging further conversation, but Natalie's aloofness didn't deter Suzanne.

"I was wondering if you ever heard strange noises when you lived at Lindenwood? There are some really weird things going on around here."

Natalie froze. Her heart began to race. She stuttered in the phone. "I-I would rather not say, Suzanne. P-Please don't call me again."

Natalie felt the breath leave her body as she eased the phone back down on the receiver. She still feared Devon and what he might be capable of doing. Had he coaxed his new fiancé into calling her in an effort to find out what she knew about the Bradford family? She wanted nothing more of Lindenwood or Devon Bradford.

Natalie's hands trembled. She felt a chill and whispered aloud. "Suzanne will just have to find out on her own. The end is always in the beginning…"

The End, for now.

*L.*Sydney Fisher

*"I first witnessed the paranormal at the tender age of eight. This experience unlocked a doorway to a world full of unexplained mysteries, miraculous insights, and terrifying ghostly visits that have spanned a lifetime. Join me as I explore these stories…one book at a time." ~*L. Sydney Fisher

Find Sydney on the WEB~

Http://www.LSydneyFisher.com

Have you heard about this story?

A story inspired by the real life Mississippi Mystic, Seymour Prater. Known throughout the South for his mysterious and miraculous abilities, he could "see" beyond the barriers of time and space while identifying a man's killer, finding stolen objects, and even locating lost people. Seymour Prater left behind a supernatural legacy and one unsolved murder that terrified a Mississippi town as the community battled their fears of the living and a dead man's ghost that haunted the 'Old Floyd Place'.

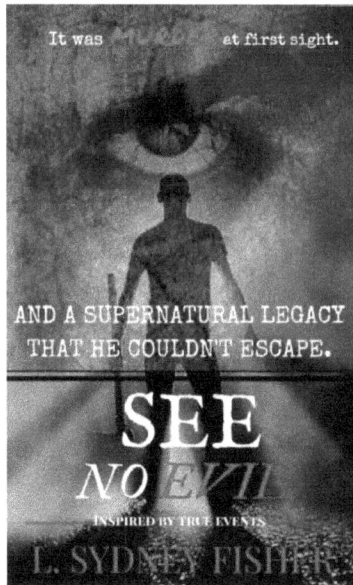

Dear Reader,

If you enjoyed this book, please consider posting a review. Reviews help authors, and I would be most grateful for your comments.

I hope you will join me again on another supernatural adventure.

Until then,

L. Sydney Fisher